Practical Ikigai

*A Guide for the Japanese Art of Unlocking
Your Best Life, Relieving Anxiety, Ending
the Struggle, and Discovering Your
Happiness & Purpose*

Allen Richardson

1

First edition

ISBN: 978-1-957337-07-4

Table of Contents

As a way to thank you for your purchase of PRACTICAL IKIGAI, I'm offering a free companion workbook: PRACTICAL IKIGAI DISCOVERY JOURNAL, for FREE to my readers.

To get instant access just go to:

hellomulberryavenue.com/ikigaidiscovery

Inside the book you will find:

- Writing prompts to explore your IKIGAI
- The core concepts described in this book
- Activities to help you better understand and drive yourself

If you want the opportunity to practice the concepts along with this book, make sure to grab the free electronic copy. Alternatively, if you would like to have the physical copy to write in directly, it can be purchased alongside wherever you purchased this book.

Introduction

Become the person you were meant to be, light your inner fire and follow your heart's desire.

— Leon Brown

Discover Your Inner Flame

To start a fire, you need three components: oxygen, heat, and fuel. The air supplies the oxygen, the matchstick (flint & friction) supplies the heat, and the fuel keeps the fire burning. Remove any of these components and you will not have a fire, or your fire will be extinguished.

This analogy can be a useful tool when addressing your own personal development. Imagine the fire burning within you. This fire was set alight at the very beginning of your life and must be sustained until the very end. This inner fire can be described as the destiny or life path each person is given, which naturally reveals itself as the fire gains size, heat and energy over many years.

During different seasons of life, the intensity of the fire changes. In some seasons it burns fervently and illuminates the whole body, and in other seasons it dims to a point where its fiery passion may barely be felt or seen. In other words, there are times in life when we may feel disconnected to who we are and struggle to find peace, stability and a sense of meaning in our lives. The key to maintaining vibrance throughout, though, is to keep the fire burning. This means having a sufficient supply of oxygen, heat and fuel to keep our inner fire ablaze.

1. **Oxygen is the setting that allows us to ignite.** Oxygen supplies a suitable environment for a flame to burn. Our surroundings and our mindset provide the appropriate conditions for us to thrive. Starting a campfire at the bottom of a lake won't get the job done and it'll just bother the fish.

2. **Heat is our passion and desire to set things in motion and bring about transformation.** It's what gets you going, what motivates, what provides the drive to take on challenges, to start new things, to overcome and to enjoy. It's the spark that comes from within us.

3. **Fuel is what sustains and keeps the inner fire burning bright.** To ensure we don't run out of fuel, we must redefine what happiness,

success and peace look and feel like for us, and be courageous enough to chase after the things that bring us maximum value. With the right fuel we can turn our lone candlestick into a brilliant blaze.

The Japanese philosophy of Ikigai can help you discover and maintain your inner flame. One way to describe Ikigai is as the reason for being that each person is born with. It can help individuals answer the questions: *Who am I? And why am I here?* The philosophy is said to have come from Okinawa, an island in Japan where locals have traditionally spent much of their lives engaging in meaningful pursuits, reconnecting with nature, and maintaining community.

It's not necessary for you to travel to Okinawa in search of your Ikigai. It's not a place or a people. Your Ikigai is within you. Finding it is a matter of quieting your mind to block out all the distractions. Conversely, it's also a matter of raising the volume of certain aspects of your mind to better listen to yourself so you can find it. Unfortunately, many of us have had our "reasons for being" muted by upbringing, societal conditioning and other outside factors that influence what we think of as meaningful.

Generally speaking, reason for being can be broken

down into 10 objectives:

1. Delighting in who you are and what you have.

2. Discovering and developing natural talents.

3. Creating meaningful work.

4. Nourishing your mind, body, and soul.

5. Connecting to the world and nature.

6. Providing value to your workplace, family, and community.

7. Serving others with your resources.

8. Healing others by offering encouragement.

9. Teaching to transfer knowledge.

10. Building a legacy that will one day outlive us.

These objectives serve as a guideline, or base to lay out, in discovering and applying your purpose. They are intentionally general. Each of us has the opportunity to choose which we decide to focus on and how to define and discover the specifics, which could make it a daunting task. It doesn't happen automatically or instantly. Finding your Ikigai is not an overnight process, nor would you really want it to be. Exploring your purpose should be an enjoyable, epic adventure.

It's called "life".

As you take the journey to reconnect to who you are and discover your inner flame, you will go through a process of change. This isn't the kind of change you should be afraid of because it brings more clarity and a sense of purpose in your life.

Anybody, regardless of age, culture, race, religion, or gender, can benefit from finding their Ikigai. The fact is that unless you feel aligned to your sense of purpose, your life will feel void of meaning. You will wake up, go about your ordinary routine and go to sleep having felt no resonance to what you are doing or how you are living. This happens to far too many of us far too often. You deserve to feel glad to be alive and energized by the small and big tasks you choose to perform each day.

If you have picked up this book, you are the perfect candidate to practice the philosophy of Ikigai. You are curious enough to embrace new ideas about how to improve your quality of life, and courageous enough to make the necessary decisions to steer your life toward your heart's desires. After reading this book, you will feel confident to pursue your passions, regardless of what others may say or the challenges that you may face along the way. Your Ikigai will drive you forward toward your destiny and bring joy and good health in your life.

Without further ado, let's begin this journey in the search for your Ikigai.

Part 1:

The Meaning and Value of Ikigai

Chapter 1:

The Origin of Ikigai

Our ikigai is different for each of us, but one thing we have in common is that we are all searching for meaning.

— Hector Garcia Puigcerver

What makes you feel glad to be alive?

In this chapter you will learn:

- The meaning and origin of Ikigai.

- The link between Ikigai and Kodawari.

- Several practical terms related to the philosophy of Ikigai.

"Ee-Key-Guy"

Ikigai, pronounced *ee-key-guy*, is a Japanese word composed of two parts. The first part, "iki", is short for *ikiru*, which is a verb that means "to live." As an adjective, it means to be alive, and as a noun it simply means "life." The second part of the word Ikigai is "gai", which originally comes from the word "kai," meaning shell. The word kai dates back to the Heian period, between 794 AD and 1185, when the Heian people considered a shell to be a prized possession. Hence, gai is commonly translated as "worth." As a complete word, Ikigai means the intrinsic value, or worth, that a person finds in their life. In the West, this would be equivalent to purpose, or the "raison d'etre" (reason for being) as the French say.

When you find your Ikigai, you find your sense of purpose. Your sense of purpose doesn't need to apply to specific areas of your life, like finding your ideal career. You can think of it in a broader sense, reflecting on various talents or characteristics you have, people you meet, tasks you perform, and passions you are invested in, which all add value to your life.

Furthermore, Ikigai doesn't necessarily refer to a spiritual experience, although it can for some. For instance, one person may use the concepts of purpose and destiny interchangeably to refer to a predetermined life path assigned to them by a higher power. But someone else may interpret the concept of purpose as being grounded in who they are as an individual, without making any spiritual references.

The philosophy of Ikigai is said to have come from ancient principles of traditional Japanese medicine. These principles emphasized the relationship between mind and body. When a person's mental health was poor, for example, it would affect their physical well-being, and vice versa. Therefore, someone who had not found their life's purpose could eventually feel overwhelmed by the push-and-pull of life and be at risk of developing physical illness, accompanied by conditions of anxiety, hypertension or chronic stress.

Psychologist Michiko Kumano has described Ikigai as a state of well-being that arises whenever someone is doing activities they enjoy or find meaningful (Gaines, 2020). Essentially, as a reward for doing purposeful tasks, the mind releases endorphins that make you feel positive about who you are and how you are utilizing your time. Kumano also distinguishes Ikigai from a fleeting feeling of pleasure (like the pleasure of digging into that ice-cream sundae), and instead associates it with a deeper sense of fulfillment that one feels about one's life. In essence, finding your Ikigai brings long-lasting happiness, not short-term gratification. In this way, it would be more appropriate to connect Ikigai with contented fulfillment, rather than pleasure.

Ikigai and Longevity

Scientists and sociologists have researched the claims that practicing the philosophy of Ikigai makes a person live longer. In 2017, a team from the Japanese TV show called *Takeshi no Katei no Igaku*, joined forces with a team of scientists to conduct research in a Japanese town called Kyotango, which is famous for having a large number of residents over 100 years old. The researchers followed seven seniors in their late 90s to early 100s to run blood tests and observe their daily routines (Dayman, 2020).

The results showed that all seven seniors had high amounts of DHEA in their blood. DHEA is a hormone produced by the adrenal glands that strengthens the immune system and can improve mental and physical well-being. In terms of common lifestyle choices, the researchers observed that all seven seniors had at least one hobby they were extremely passionate about, which they practiced on a daily basis. Thus, the researchers were able to conclude that having something you are genuinely interested in can increase your sense of fulfillment in life and increase the amounts of DHEA your body secretes, which can lead to a longer and satisfying life.

Author Dan Buettner in his book titled, *Blue Zones: Lessons on Living Longer from the People Who've Lived the Longest*, studied a few locations around the world with high populations of centenarians, like Sardinia in Italy, Icaria in Greece and Okinawa in Japan. Interestingly, what seniors in these communities all had in common was the exposure to warm weather with plenty of sun, consuming a healthy plant-based diet, and living a purpose-driven lifestyle (Beuttner, 2010). While sunshine and physical health are, of course, key to a long life, engaging in meaning-infused daily practices are also essential to longevity.

Nevertheless, the concept of Ikigai should not be inextricably linked with old age because even though senior citizens in many parts of the world live by this philosophy, it can be equally, if not more, commonly practiced by younger generations of people, whether they be young adults or those who are in their midlife. In fact, people of all ages participate in Ikigai, whether they are actively and consciously doing it or not. Moreover, the concept of Ikigai is not only practiced in Japan or in the Mediterranean, but in many countries around the world.

The Principle of Kodawari

Think back to a time when you felt a strong conviction to do something. It could've been a New Year's resolution or an unexpected "Aha" moment that got you excited. You may have felt your energy and focus rise to an all-time high and been inspired to make a positive change.

But how long did your "high" last? A few days, weeks, or months?

What we often rely on when completing daily tasks or pursuing goals is motivation. The only problem with being fueled by motivation is that it tends to diminish as the excitement of the idea wears off and we are forced to contend with the reality of overcoming everyday obstacles. Instead of relying on short bursts of motivation to drive you in pursuit of your goals, you can consider another Japanese concept, known as Kodawari.

Kodawari is the pursuit of excellence or mastery. It is about committing to your words and actions and paying close attention to the intricacies of each task you perform. Practicing Kodawari requires more discipline and persistence than riding the wave of motivation. You focus your attention on how you perform something because it is through a method or process that mastery can take place.

Kodawari forms an integral part of Ikigai. If your Ikigai is the meaning you derive from your life, then Kodawari is what helps you maintain the kind of standards you have set for your life. Of course, each individual's standards will look different, so how each person applies Kodawari won't look the same either. What matters is the personal pride you get when you check off each daily task on your list, make an improvement in even a small way or go to bed every night knowing that you have done your best.

You can also see Kodawari as being the voice of your conscience that alerts you when you are cutting corners or behave in ways that don't honor who you are. What makes this voice powerful is the fact that it knows just how far you can go and how much you are capable of achieving. Therefore, Kodawari makes your life's journey feel significant and it reminds you that true purpose is found in the process or day-to-day life affairs, not in reaching the outcome.

The desired outcome or goal is the target we are trying to reach, and without it we are aimless. However, at the end of the day, it's the journey, the process, the tasks and activities that make it all worthwhile. So, it is important, in fact essential, to ensure the time, energy, planning and doing bring satisfaction and/or enjoyment. It's the "going there", not the "getting there".

There are many inspirational leaders in the world who embody the principle of Kodawari. Take, for example, Gary Vaynerchuk, best-selling author, marketing guru and super-star entrepreneur. Gary V. has a relentless commitment to his company, VaynerMedia. He found his Ikigai in creating innovative media that inspired millions. However, in finding his Ikigai, he also demonstrates Kodawari by seeking to push the boundaries of conventional wisdom and continuously modifying his approach to doing business.

Like a true practitioner of Kodawari, Gary V. knows that he will never really be "done" or reach a point where he has fully maximized his potential. In each new project he undertakes he is able to build upon his existing knowledge and resources in the endless pursuit of legacy. His love of process and action embody the spirit of Kodawari. In his own words: "Love the journey… If you don't love the journey then you will never get through the first quarter".

Ikigai in Practical Terms

Although the meaning of Ikigai has been adapted

throughout the centuries, the essence of it hasn't been lost. Nonetheless, since your Ikigai can look completely different from my Ikigai, it's important that we look at various terms that can explain this philosophy so that we can have a better understanding of the different ways it can be practiced in everyday life. Here are three practical terms that describe Ikigai:

1. Reason to Live/Reason for Being

When something is your reason for living, it explains your existence. It is an essential aspect of who you are that you place at the center of your life. On a fundamental level, your Ikigai is the crux of who you are. It is what makes your existence feel worthwhile.

2. Purpose for Life

Your purpose for life is the goal or vision that keeps you motivated to live your life to the fullest. It is the reason you wake up each morning and soldier through every obstacle you face in life. Your purpose can also act as a guiding force through life, causing you to focus on those tasks, activities, and interests that are aligned to your goals. Your Ikigai can provide you with a sense of purpose and influence your character, behaviors, career and relationships.

3. Meaning of Life

The meaning of life refers to the significance you ascribe to life. In other words, it explains what you believe life is meant to be about. The significance you ascribe to your life will be closely related to your purpose. In other words, if you believe that your purpose is to heal others through an art form, you might believe that life is all about finding and honing your natural talent then sharing it with others to improve society at large. You could also believe that life is all about finding your Ikigai or practicing Kodawari, or any other positive discipline.

5 Pillars of Ikigai

At this point, we know that Ikigai can be defined as one's reason for being, but what we haven't discussed are the things one needs to do to find their reason for being. Throughout this book, I will share with you various strategies to find your Ikigai, which are in part based on the five pillars of Ikigai: starting small, releasing yourself, creating harmony and sustainability, finding joy in the little things, and being in the here and now. These five pillars are outlined in the book titled, *The Little Book of Ikigai*, written by author and neuroscientist Ken Moagi. I recommend you read it if you have the chance. Here is an overview of the five pillars:

1. Start Small

Moagi associates the first pillar of starting small with the principle of Kodawari. When you practice Ikigai, you must consider how you desire it to show up in every aspect of your life, hence the need to start small. Taking baby steps toward your goals can make you more intentional about how you plan on spending every minute of your day. You can focus on making change at a micro-level, by adjusting how you structure your day. Even though there is no such thing as a perfect day, much less a perfect life, the amount of effort it takes to strive for perfection can bring positive results in your life—one purposeful step at a time.

2. Release Yourself

What is meant by "releasing yourself?" When you release yourself you accept yourself for who you are. This requires a level of self-awareness whereby you identify your strengths and weaknesses and come to a sober realization about what you like and dislike, the things you are good at or passionate about, and the core values and principles that help you navigate your life. Releasing yourself also involves challenging your old conditioning, including the ideas and beliefs you were taught as a child which may or may not align with who you are or how you desire to live your life. By doing this, you release yourself from societal expectations and external validation, so you can gain or regain control over your life.

3. Creating Harmony and Sustainability

Harmony refers to the coming together of different parts to form a cohesive and consistent flow and combination. Sustainability on the other hand refers to the ability to maintain the flow or balance in your life. When you decide to practice Ikigai, it becomes the glue that brings consistency and order in different parts of your life. All of your goals, regardless of how different they may be, guide you toward a common goal or vision—which is your Ikigai. However, your goals or activities must also be sustainable, meaning that they must contribute to bringing value not only in your life but also to your family and community.

4. Finding Joy in the Little Things

One of the central themes of Ikigai is gratitude. Gratitude can be described as showing appreciation for what you have. The reason practicing gratitude is so important is that it enhances your quality of life and makes each moment feel meaningful. By changing your outlook on your life, you can derive a sense of joy from your daily tasks. In other words, once you reframe how you perceive yourself and your surroundings, your perception of your life will positively improve. There are some people who believe that in order to incorporate Ikigai in their lives, they need to make drastic changes to their routines. However, all it takes to see and feel positive improvements is a mental shift.

5. Being in the Here and Now

The fifth and final pillar is being in the here and now. In the Buddhist tradition, this is known as the practice of mindfulness. Mindfulness refers to bringing your awareness to the present moment instead of splitting your focus to past events or future possibilities. The only real time you have is this moment, so paying attention to your present experiences can enhance your quality of life. Being here and now also opens you up to an infinite number of possibilities. Just think about the infinite number of ideas, activities, and plans you could be working on right now. When you practice being in the moment, you can activate your creative brain, confront whatever negative thought or emotion that arises, calibrate your life, and devote yourself to continuous learning.

In the upcoming chapters, you will notice these pillars mentioned again when explaining the various strategies for practicing Ikigai. In your personal reflection time, you can think about these pillars and the ways in which they manifest in your life.

Chapter Takeaways

- Ikigai is the intrinsic value you assign to your life.

- Although it is a Japanese philosophy, it is practiced throughout the world, across multiple generations of people.

- Kodawari, the principle of pursuing mastery, can help you maintain the standards you set in your life and keep you accountable to your goals.

- Ikigai is personal in nature and can look different for each individual.

Now that you have been introduced to the idea of finding your life's worth, the next step is to understand some of the misconceptions about Ikigai that create false expectations.

Chapter 2:

Misconceptions—

What Ikigai Is Not

Wealth does not mean a person who owns a lot, but refers to someone who has enough time to enjoy what nature and human collaboration place within everyone's reach.

— Franco Bifo Berardi

Can you define the value you add to others without mentioning your job?

In this chapter you will learn:

- How the Western version of Ikigai differs from the traditional Japanese meaning of Ikigai.

- Common myths related to Ikigai that are misleading.

- How to live your Ikigai when you haven't found your passion.

The Purpose Venn Diagram

The Western version of Ikigai is based on a diagram created by Spanish author and astrologer Andres Zuzunaga, known as the Purpose Venn Diagram. The diagram represents four components to achieving Ikigai:

1. Finding what you love

2. Finding what the world needs

3. Finding what you are good at

4. Finding what you can get paid for

Here is a brief explanation of each component:

1. Finding What You Love

When seeking to find what you love, you look for experiences that bring joy into your life and make you feel alive. What you love could be a hobby that you are passionate about, working on self-improvement, or spending quality time with friends and family. What you love doesn't have to be something you're good at or something that makes you money.

2. Finding What the World Needs

You can define your "world" as your family, community, or any interest group you identify with. Finding what the world needs requires you to put others' needs before your own and find ways of serving people with your natural talents and skills. Your contribution to the world doesn't have to be big, as long as it is meaningful and makes a difference in someone else's life.

3. Finding What You Are Good At

There are certain gifts or skills that you possess that can be developed and make your life more fulfilling. When you are good at doing something, you can excel at it without much effort. Moreover, with practice and determination you can turn your talents and skills into financial opportunities. Even if you don't make money from your talents and skills, you can still find ways to share them with the world.

4. Finding What You Can Get Paid For

A central theme to the western version of Ikigai is turning purpose into profit. That is why this fourth component is so important. When you seek to monetize your passions, you must consider the market value of what you have to offer. In other words, you should ask yourself whether people would be willing to pay for your passion. You might be passionate about a particular hobby, like creating mosaics, but that doesn't mean that people would be willing to pay you for it. Therefore, according to the Purpose Venn Diagram, passions worth pursuing are those that are in high demand and can offer monetary returns.

These four components intersect with each other to creative sub-goals:

- Where "what you love" and "what you are good at" intersect, you get your passion.

- Where "what you love" and "what the world needs" intersect, you get your mission.

- Where "what the world needs" and "what you can get paid for" intersect, you get your vocation.

- Where "what you are good at" and "what you can get paid for" intersect, you get your profession.

According to the diagram, your Ikigai would be the sum of what you love, what you are good at, what the world needs, and what you can get paid for. For example, if you love people, are a trained nurse, work at a hospital, and you get paid for it, you could say that you have found your Ikigai.

However, there has been a lot of debate around this Purpose Venn Diagram, particularly as it relates to the authentic Japanese meaning of Ikigai. For instance, the diagram suggests that to find your Ikigai, you must meet all four conditions. This means that if you have found what you love but can't monetize it or can't find a need for it in the world, then it can't be considered your Ikigai. This is very different from the traditional meaning of Ikigai that has very little to do with money or subjective value. Traditionally, Ikigai doesn't need to be anything you get paid to do or anything that is a talent. In fact, the move to monetize or profit from your Ikigai can be, although not necessarily, a hindrance to achieving satisfaction in what you do. In some cases, profit can be a helpful motivator and a fruitful passion in itself depending on the person, circumstance, etc. However, the "getting paid" aspect should not be seen as a necessary component of Ikigai.

Generally, those successful at living their Ikigai don't abide by these four components and they certainly don't consider them to be central to finding purpose and living a meaningful life. Nevertheless, the diagram is useful to some extent because it has opened the world to Ikigai in a concise way, clearly identifying the interconnection between affinity, ability, and value. An example of this is the many insightful self-reflective questions that you can ask yourself pertaining to the four components, such as:

1. Questions About Finding What You Love

Here are a few self-reflective questions you can ask yourself about what you love:

- What do you find most important in life?

- What are some of your core values, and how do you practice them every day?

- Who are the people you enjoy spending time with?

- What makes you happy?

- What are some of the things you find beautiful?

- What calms your mind and body?

2. Questions About Finding What the World Needs

You can also ask yourself questions related to how you can help others:

- What do people often consult with you about?

- What do you believe the world is lacking that you have in abundance?

- What legacy would you like to leave behind?

- How could you play an active role in your community?

- How can you contribute to others?

3. Questions About Finding What You Are Good At

These questions will help you identify some of your hidden abilities that you can point you toward your Ikigai:

- What activities do you enjoy doing in your spare time?

- What skills come easy for you?

- What are the achievements you have obtained throughout your life?

- What skills do you get the most recognition about?

- What does success mean for you?

4. Questions About Finding What You Can Get Paid For

Although the traditional meaning of Ikigai doesn't describe purpose as being connected to financial gain, there are a few questions you can ask yourself pertaining to your work that can help you find your Ikigai:

- If money wasn't a factor, what would you spend your time doing?

- What kind of work environment would you feel satisfied in?

- What values do you find important in a workplace?

- What does the world or your community value?

- What value can you bring to others?

Myths About Ikigai

Since there are different interpretations of Ikigai, the essence of this traditional philosophy can get lost in translation. It's therefore important to recognize what Ikigai is and what it isn't so that you can successfully integrate principles of Ikigai into your life. Here are common myths pertaining to Ikigai that provide an incorrect understanding of the philosophy:

Myth 1: Ikigai Is About Finding Work You Are Passionate About

Ikigai isn't necessarily related to the kind of work you do or your job. Just think about it: If the true meaning of Ikigai is the reason for being, is it fair to say that you were born to work? Of course, work offers you financial stability and finding the right work can make you happier, but your career isn't the reason why you are alive. A 2010 survey was done with 2,000 Japanese men and women, and only 31% of the respondents defined their Ikigai as the work they do (Mitsuhashi, 2017). Therefore, while work can be considered a person's Ikigai, it isn't true for everybody. There are other aspects of life people may find meaningful, such as family, health, travel, or social responsibility and charitable giving.

Myth 2: Ikigai Is Your Sole Life Purpose

There are some who believe that your Ikigai is the one only life purpose that you have. This kind of belief can make finding your Ikigai feel overwhelming. After all, who really knows where to begin to find their one and only life purpose? And if you do choose one and only one life purpose, it would follow that you must also cease with all other pursuits and focus devotedly to your one exclusive purpose.

The truth is that your Ikigai can evolve over time, as you grow and learn. Think of it as a central theme that you carry in your life, which can manifest as different interests, activities, and goals across the many life stages you will go through. For example, if your central theme is healing, you can find various jobs, interests, and goals that carry an element of healing as you grow and learn. As you change, and as the world around you changes, so will your Ikigai.

Myth 3: I Have to Quit My Job or Start a Business to Live My Ikigai

Ikigai can sometimes be confused as a gateway to entrepreneurship or freelancing. Since Ikigai isn't necessarily related to the job that you do, you don't have to make a career transition or live a nomadic lifestyle to live your Ikigai. You can find ways to enrich your life while still maintaining your current obligations and responsibilities.

Myth 4: Practicing the Philosophy of Ikigai Is Selfish

Ikigai is far from being selfish. In fact, it is the most altruistic way of living your life. When you find your reason for being, you can make a significant contribution in the lives of those around you. You have a greater sense of self-awareness, which makes you sensitive to your role and responsibility to your family, neighborhood, workplace, and country. Ikigai helps you find your unique place in the world and identify the most meaningful way you can make a contribution to others.

Myth 5: I'm Too Young/Old to Live My Ikigai

You can find your Ikigai at any age and apply it to your life in an age-appropriate manner. For instance, how a person in their late 70s lives their Ikigai will look different from how a person in their late 30s or even a teenager lives their Ikigai. The philosophy remains the same in each case, but the meaning that each individual ascribes to their life differs. It is also true that age isn't the best benchmark to assess how well a person is living their Ikigai—it is better to assess the amount of fulfillment they receive as a result of living their Ikigai.

You Are Not Your Job

It's easy for us to get caught up in the trap of identifying with our work. For instance, instead of someone saying "I'm in banking" they will say "I am a banker." Even though we tend to do it unconsciously, it comes with many implications about how we see ourselves and the value we have to offer.

For example, Tim identifies himself as a banker and believes that to succeed in his career he needs to be ambitious, extroverted and competitive. Since these aren't his natural traits, he needs to learn new behaviors that align with his profession. After some time, Tim adapts to the expectations that come with his career field and slowly starts disconnecting from his true self. Even worse, he gets so blinded by the external expectations of his job that he carries over these learned behaviors and attitudes into other parts of his life too. Eventually, every aspect of Tim's life becomes centered or influenced by his work—nothing else.

Does this sound familiar? It may not be a reflection of your own life, but you may know someone who has become so wrapped up in their work that it has taken over their lives. This kind of devotion to work isn't healthy because it makes it difficult for the individual to distinguish between who they are and what they do for a living. From a young age, the line between who a person is and what they do is blurred. Children are groomed to one day identify with their profession.

Asking a child: "What do you want to be when you grow up?" causes them to associate identity with a chosen career field. After years of being conditioned to think this way, young adults embrace the idea that a single career choice can make or break their future. The pressure to choose the right career field is immense because no young person wants to regret identifying with the wrong profession. What they are not told is that what they do has no bearing on who they are, and the failure to secure a good job isn't a reflection of their own inadequacies.

Perhaps the main issue with identifying with your work is that you are not in control of your career prospects. How far you advance in your company, how much money you make, or the career opportunities you are exposed to are to a large degree out of your control. If things start going badly at work, your industry takes a dive, or you aren't making as much money as you would've hoped for, it can feel like a personal failure. Thus, you end up giving work an incredible amount of power over your mental and emotional well-being.

Author Malcolm Harris wrote a book titled *Kids These Days: Human Capital and the Making of Millennials.* In the book, he speaks about the burden of the capitalist system on millennials (defined as people born between 1980 and 2000). He investigates why millennials are so burned out and why they are starting families later in life. Harris argued that certain toxic capitalist traditions, like competition among workers, increased isolation of workers, and extreme individualism in Western society had a lot to do with it. In an interview with journalist Sean Illing, Harris said: "Our entire lives are framed around becoming cheaper and more efficient economic instruments for capital. That, taken to an extreme, has pretty corrosive effects on society, particularly young people" (Illing, 2019).

One might argue that workers aren't given much of a choice when it comes to making their jobs an important aspect of their lives. Some companies, for example, demand an exceptional amount of dedication from their workers, which makes it hard to focus on anything else. However, it is still an individual choice whether a person will center their life around work or center their work around their life, particularly in the long term.

You Are Not the Amount of Money

You Make

It goes without saying that we all need money to survive; however, how well we thrive is not solely dependent on money. While having enough money is important, making it the purpose of your existence can cause you to neglect other areas of your life, such as your health and relationships, which provide more value than money.

Of course, having more money can improve a person's quality of life, which may lead to greater feelings of satisfaction. A number of studies have been done on this, as if you needed them for convincing. However, the link between having a lot of money and positive mental and emotional well-being isn't a strong one. For example, economist Richard Easterlin studied the effects of an increase in standard of living and a household's level of happiness. He found that a majority of the household income went toward basic necessities, like shelter, food, and healthcare. The remainder of the money that was spent on luxury items. The purchasing and owning of these items didn't bring a significant amount of pleasure scientifically speaking. What actually made households "happy" was the ability to afford their lifestyle and sustain their livelihoods. Households that made $100,000 per year were only marginally more satisfied than households that made $50,000, not doubly (Spoto, 2021). Thus, there is a certain tipping point at which the richer a household becomes, the less effect their income has on their well-being.

Another study that looked at data from the Korean General Social Survey over a three-year period wanted to see if there was a relationship between personal values and happiness. The results of the study showed that respondents who prioritized spirituality were most likely to be happy, followed by respondents who prioritized social relationships with relatives, friends, and neighbors. Respondents who were least likely to be happy were those who prioritized extrinsic achievements, such as power, money, social status, work, and education. The study concluded that prioritizing goals related to self-enhancement results in less satisfaction than prioritizing goals related to self-transcendence or the needs of the group (Lee & Kawachi, 2019).

There are many other things more valuable in this world than the pursuit of money. Here are just a few:

1. Good Health

What is the purpose of being alive if you aren't mentally and physically well? How can you enjoy each day of your life when you are waking up in mental or physical pain? Health is more valuable than money because there is no amount of money in the world that can reverse severe illnesses. The best way to protect yourself from chronic disease is to live a healthy lifestyle—which is more affordable than the alternative. It is only through your healthy habits, such as living an active lifestyle, eating healthfully, and getting enough sleep that you can reduce the risk of getting sick.

2. Community

Having a solid support system is more valuable than money because human beings cannot live for long periods in isolation from others. We need positive connections with people more than we need a million dollars. Being part of a community can improve your health and give you support. You can also exchange ideas and knowledge with your community members, which can assist you in achieving your goals. As the African proverb says, "If you want to go fast, go alone. If you want to go far, go together."

3. Time

What is the one thing that money can't buy? Time. Time is a limited resource because once it is gone, it can never be returned. Unlike money, you can't multiply time or borrow it from someone else. You will never be younger than you are right now. You may never experience a day similar to the one you are currently living. It's therefore important to find ways of managing your time wisely, being intentional with how you desire to live your life and ceasing your days.

4. Respect

Having respect for all that is grand in the world, for others, for those that came before breeds an appreciation for what we have and what we can become. It allows us to be humble enough to learn from others and the past. It enables us to acknowledge what is valuable.

On the flip side, being respected by others is something that we all desire. Because we are social creatures, we need others to trust us in order to build and maintain healthy relationships. Without trust, there can be no respect—and vice versa. Similar to time, you can't buy respect, and once it is gone, it is very difficult to reestablish it. Being a respectable person can increase your personal value and make it easier to form healthy connections with others.

5. Mental Toughness

Mental toughness is the ability to remain resilient during difficult times and push past your failures.

Mental toughness is more valuable than money because it gives you your "staying power" and helps you achieve your goals. As long as you don't give up, you are bound to succeed, even if you experience a few setbacks. Mental toughness can also help you learn from your failures, regulate your emotions, and adopt an optimistic outlook on life. Therefore, having mental toughness is what makes success possible.

Imperfect Ikigai

Very few people are able to achieve full Ikigai in every aspect of their lives, all the time. That's okay. You might not be passionate about your job or some other aspect of your daily routine. You might still need to develop your skills and talents to get to the place you want to be in life. You might not be living a perfectly balanced lifestyle where your Ikigai is firing on all cylinders non-stop. Remember that Ikigai is about the process or journey of experiencing a meaningful life, not the destination. Therefore, your Ikigai will always look incomplete to some degree because your life is still, and always will be, a work in progress. No matter how far you think you may be from achieving your Ikigai, remind yourself that your Ikigai cannot be lost—it is the core of who you are and with time and growth, it will be revealed.

Even with a well-established Ikigai you'll still have bad days. You'll still have aspects of your life that you are dissatisfied with. You'll still experience failure. And due to circumstances, often outside of your control, you may find that fully incorporating Ikigai into every nook and cranny of your every moment just isn't possible. That's ok. Do what you can. Some is better than none. It's ok to not be hitting home runs at every at bat. Doubles, singles, bunts, walks are all fine. And if you swing and miss a couple or hit a foul ball, well, at least you're still at the plate.

When you get discouraged during the process of finding your Ikigai, turn the word into a verb. Think of your Ikigai as being something that you do and let that inspire you to take action. In other words, your Ikigai can be something you create, build, learn, influence, or express. Thinking of it in these terms broadens your understanding of what your purpose could be in each stage of your life. It represents the simplest form of how you can positively change your life and impact the world.

Plus, the verb(s) you use for your Ikigai can change as your life circumstances change. For example, if you are stuck in a job that you dislike and don't have any hope of resigning, you can see your Ikigai as being "to persevere." Each morning when you wake up to prepare for work, you remind yourself that your main objective or mission in this particular stage in your life is to persevere. At work, you could adopt coping strategies that can improve your level of patience and tolerance. Even outside of work, you can adopt healthy habits that reinforce the theme of perseverance, such as playing a sport or enrolling in a short course. By doing this, you can turn an imperfect Ikigai into a meaningful Ikigai, without overhauling your life.

Below is a list of different verbs you can use to define your Ikigai. Feel free to choose as many verbs as you deem appropriate to help you along your journey:

- Accelerate

- Amplify

- Build

- Connect

- Create

- Excel

- Express

- Improvise

- Integrate

- Overcome

- Transcend

- Understand

In a sense, Ikigai is not something you are or have or get. It's something you do.

Chapter Takeaways

- The Western idea of Ikigai seeks to monetize your purpose. This is different from how the Japanese interpret Ikigai, which has very little to do with financial profit.

- While some people may define their Ikigai as career-related, not everyone derives a sense of purpose from their work. Moreover, it's possible to continue living your Ikigai even if you aren't passionate about your job.

- As you grow and learn, your Ikigai will evolve to adapt to your current lifestyle needs, interests, and goals. Nevertheless, the central theme of your purpose will remain the same throughout various seasons of your life.

- Your Ikigai does not need to be perfect.

You have a solid understanding of what Ikigai is and what it isn't. The next step is to show you how you can maintain your Ikigai in the long-term by understanding the three drivers of Ikigai: passion, capacity and community.

Chapter 3:

The Drivers to Living Your Ikigai

There is no passion to be found playing small--in settling for a life that is less than the one you are capable of living.

— Nelson Mandela

What helps you get in your flow?

In this chapter you will learn:

- How to enter and maintain your unique "flow."

- The steps to turn your passion into your purpose.

- The difference between talent and skill, and how to leverage them!

- The importance of community and ways to share your value with others.

- The number one barrier that can make it difficult to live in Ikigai.

Achieving Your Flow State

Some of us are in desperate need of a fresh start. Some of us spend most of our lives seeking after what others wanted for us, not what we wanted for ourselves. In this case it can be important to make adjustments and reestablish who we are, which can be daunting. But it can also be liberating because it allows us to find ourselves.

Finding your Ikigai is like finding your special flow. We all have a flow, or rhythm, that we naturally follow as we engage in various activities and navigate our lives; however, many of us are not aware of it. Finding your flow helps determine precisely what you find interesting, how you see the world, and how you can inject life with meaning.

Picture the movement of water rushing down a steep mountain or waterfall. The water flows because it cannot stay in one place unless it is contained. It finds its path naturally, without struggle. Its continuous flow purifies and sustains life.

Finding your flow can create a sense of calmness inside of you. Instead of dividing your attention on scattered thoughts and conflicting aims, focus only on those few things that allow you to get into your flow. Without the proper focus and intention our minds and actions can get muddied and stagnant. Getting through the day and whatever tasks we take on can be a grind.

The same applies when we are ready to embrace our Ikigai. We need to define our own personal purpose and be intentional about key decisions we make (practicing Kodawari). The concept of purpose is broad, but when applied in our own lives, it is customized to suit our individual and particular needs, values, and beliefs. Therefore, reminding yourself to maintain your special flow helps define what Ikigai can mean for you, and personalize the whole experience.

There are three drivers of Ikigai that can help you find your special flow. These drivers are passion, capacity, and community. In the next three sections, we will discuss each driver and practical tips on how you can apply them in your life.

What Is Passion?

Passion is a strong desire for something and an intense energy to pursue it. You can think of passionate lovers who have a strong pull toward each other, passionate entrepreneurs who sacrifice all of their time and money for their businesses, or passionate activists who dedicate their lives to fighting for or against certain causes.

Other words that describe passion are love, determination, and conviction. When you love something, you derive an immense amount of pleasure from it. If you are determined to accomplish something, then you readily embrace making sacrifices along the way that will help you achieve your goal. And when you have conviction about something, you hold a firm belief or opinion about it and aren't easily persuaded to think otherwise.

Although passion is a noun, in practice let's treat it like a verb. In other words, engaging in passion, acting passionately, is what sets your tasks and plans in motion, creating inertia, and makes them sustainable in the long-term. Without passion, you can find yourself living your life on autopilot, being physically present but mentally and emotionally disconnected from your routines. You may still have a stable job, family, and social life, but you aren't mentally and emotionally engaged enough to actually appreciate these various aspects of your life.

So how do you determine what you are passionate about? To answer this question, let's pose another question: *How far are you willing to go to become better at it?* When you set out to achieve any kind of goal, whether it is a health, career, or personal development goal, you will be presented with obstacles along the way. In general, the bigger the goal, the more complex these obstacles tend to be, by definition. But when you are passionate about something, you are willing to do whatever it takes to fulfill the desire, including overcoming the obstacles that come your way.

For example, Sheila and Betty may love to cook, but only one of them may be passionate about cooking. How could we test this? Well, we would simply need to find out how far they are willing to go to become better cooks. Sheila may love cooking, but only when she is in the mood to do it. She may watch some cooking shows on TV, but wouldn't go as far as paying to partake in a cooking class or buying a recipe book. Betty on the other hand is devoted to her love for cooking to the extent that she has set a standard for herself to cook every meal with love, regardless of how she might feel on a particular day. Watching cooking shows on TV isn't enough to satisfy her yearning to become a master chef one day, hence she saves up money toward cooking courses, conferences, and dining in Michelin star restaurants.

Now imagine that both Sheila and Betty were presented with an obstacle that came in the way of their love for cooking. Let's say that their kitchen stoves malfunctioned and the only way to fix the problem was to invest in a new one. How each person would handle the obstacle depends on their level of commitment toward their love for cooking. Since Betty is willing to go above and beyond for her love for cooking, we can assume that she would dig into her savings and purchase a new stove immediately. Although it would set her back financially, it is a sacrifice she is willing to make to continue making progress in her passion. Sheila may have enough money saved to purchase a new kitchen stove too, but since she isn't passionate about cooking, she may not be able to justify the expense in her mind and may delay in buying a new one.

Passion is often associated with the work that one performs. We are often told to pursue careers that we are passionate about, which means finding work that adds value to our lives. But what if circumstances force us to stay in jobs that we aren't necessarily passionate about, but value nonetheless due to the stability they provide us? This is usually when we need to consider the subjectivity of value. For example, someone might not be passionate about their role at work, but they are still willing to work hard at what they do because of the many opportunities their position can open for them. In other words, they aren't necessarily passionate about their current job but they are extremely passionate about where their job could take them in the future.

Another area where passion is often applied is the area of relationships. Once again, we are told that truly meaningful relationships can only be established with those we share similar passions with, or are passionate about. This idea can make us invest our time and energy on a few close friends and family, and turn our backs on everyone else. The reality is that we will seldom get along with everybody, particularly those people who live differently from us. However, that doesn't mean that two people who think and live differently can't add value in each other's lives. In fact, working in a team or forming a business partnership with someone who sees things differently than you can actually improve the quality of the creative thinking and decision-making processes because there is more than one perspective to consider. Therefore, you may not be necessarily passionate about a person but you can still be passionate about how the both of you can collaborate and have a positive impact on each other. You don't need to be passionate, in the platonic sense, about another person to have passion in the relationship and the value or benefit it can provide.

Much like we discussed previously with "Imperfect Ikigai", your passion can also be imperfect. It does not need to be a blazing inferno of excitement and drive for every aspect of everything in your life. If you can find even just a spark of it, even in just one piece of a larger whole, then it can be enough to ignite a flame. And candlelight can sometimes be enough to let us see what we need to.

You may not be passionate about the obvious task or activity you are performing but about the significance the task or activity brings to your life. Political activists like Nelson Mandela or Mahatma Gandhi were not necessarily passionate about being political prisoners, facing police brutality, and the many sacrifices they had to make in their pursuit for freedom and justice. Nevertheless, they endured through the hardships due to their devotion toward their causes and the significance behind their defiance campaigns.

Turning Passion Into Purpose

Wouldn't it be amazing to wake up each morning knowing you are working toward something meaningful? Or that your daily tasks will positively contribute toward achieving your goals? This is the kind of lifestyle you could live when you are living your Ikigai. Every day would bring opportunities to make progress toward your life goals and incorporate your passions into your daily tasks and activities.

Turning what you are passionate about into your purpose is the crux of Ikigai. Instead of devoting your time and energy into what you think is socially acceptable or what will gain the most approval from others, you focus your attention on the things you already find meaningful and make them the center of your life. For example, Betty, the devoted cook, could turn her passion of cooking into her life's purpose by making it the center of her life. Cooking would no longer become a mere hobby that she performs on weekends or whenever she has free time, rather, she would define her mission in life as serving others through cooking. She would also look at other ways to make her passion sustainable, such as starting a cooking school or catering business. Or she could develop her passion more concisely by, for example, committing to prepare an unique, challenging, outstanding meal for herself every Sunday evening.

If you are looking for ways to turn your passion into purpose, here are three tips that can help you:

1. Get to Know Yourself

This tip may sound overly simplified, but many of us don't prioritize introspection. For example, you may think you know yourself, but you only know of certain aspects of who you are, not the full picture. You may find yourself too busy with "life" and have not taken the time to consider what makes you tick. It can take a lifetime to discover who you truly are and what you desire in your life, especially when you have spent most of your life making decisions based on social and cultural conditioning.

When you are ready to turn your passion into purpose, you need to first figure out if what you desire is based on your genuine beliefs and wants or whether it is something else, such as the result of what others want for you. Here are a few critical questions you can think about when getting to know yourself and the motivation behind your passion:

- Think back to a time in your life when you were at a crossroads and had to pick between two major life decisions that affected your career, health, lifestyle, or relationships. Which decision did you end up taking? And what or who were the main factors that informed your decision?

- What is the one thing you strongly dislike in life? It could be human behavior, social ill, or a particular lifestyle. What is it about this thing that you don't like? Is it the harm it causes others or the environment? Or how it conflicts with your values or principles?

- Next, think about one person who you admire deeply. It could be someone you know or a person you haven't met before but who has influenced how you see or experience your life. What specifically do you admire about this person? Is it their mindset or worldview? The beliefs they stand for or their incredible resilience or work ethic?

- Take a trip down memory lane and reflect on how you spent most of your time as a child. What kind of activities would you spend hours on? What were some of your hobbies and interests? When you role-played with your friends, what role would you play, or what kind of character would you play out?

- If you had a lot more time on your hands than you currently do, what would you spend your time doing? How would you design your ultimate daily routine? Would you spend most of your time on a craft? Or would you be out and about socializing?

2. Take Your Passions Seriously

To turn a passion into your purpose, you must see it as

more than just a desire or passing thought. How can you act on your passions in a real way? Can they be developed into a pastime or hobby? A side gig? A new career?

Remember that your purpose is anything that gives your life meaning. This means that it becomes the center of who you are. You don't have to take this literally. For instance, someone who is passionate about physical exercise doesn't need to define themselves by their passion. A passion for fitness does not mean one must become the ideal model of healthy living and the perfect specimen of physicality. However, a passion for exercise should influence lifestyle choices, mindset, daily routines, and the kinds of goals aimed for.

If you want to take your passion seriously you need to understand the significance of it, and how it relates to your Ikigai. Think about the physical and psychological payoff that fulfilling your passion gives you. For example, the physical payoff for working out could be achieving a strong and healthy body and the psychological payoff could be improving self-discipline. Reminding yourself about the physical and psychological payoff will help you commit to your passion and see it as more than something you are just "good at".

3. Dream Big, But Take Baby Steps

Turning a passion into your purpose comes with its own share of risks and sacrifices. The more risk you are exposed to, or the more sacrifices are demanded, the less likely you will be to devote your time and energy on developing your passion. You can minimize the risks involved and improve your likelihood of commitment by taking things slow. Taking things slow means not rushing the planning process or turning a blind eye to the red flags. When you take your time to carefully consider how to develop your passion, you can address mistakes as they arise and test your plan on a day-to-day basis. You can also assess how your strengths and weaknesses play a factor in developing your passions, and make small adjustments to how you approach your plans.

Taking baby steps doesn't mean lowering your standards. Your standards are what help you stay focused on your purpose, so these should never drop. However, when you take baby steps you break down your goals into manageable stages or milestones and go after them incrementally. While baby steps can look different for each person, remember to avoid biting off more than you can chew. Ensure that you set tasks or make plans that you are able to implement with the strengths, skills, and resources you already have. You must also find ways to incorporate your passion in your current lifestyle and make minor adjustments until your lifestyle resembles your life's purpose.

What Is Capacity?

Capacity is the ability and potential to do something well. It could also be defined as the skill, talent, and knowledge you apply to achieving a certain goal. Your capacities tend to develop as you grow and learn. For instance, a child loses their balance and falls several times before they are able to learn how to walk. Your capacity can be limited by your level of maturation and the amount of skills or knowledge you have acquired. Anyone can desire to become a doctor, but only those who have gone to medical school and undergone the specialized training will eventually become doctors. In other words, to some degree, depending on your level of experience and knowledge, you have the ability (capacity) to perform certain tasks, while unable to perform others. It is only when you increase your level of experience and knowledge that you can improve your capacity.

Your capacity is what and how much you are able to take on. It differs for all of us. Some of us have a penchant for detail. Others may be "big picture" thinkers. Some are devoted, quick, active, experienced, etc. Others are flexible, thoughtful, stoic, creative, etc. Our capacity is both a natural inclination and skills that can be developed. Some things we are just good at automatically. While others we can train to build up.

Capacity includes both the soft skills of patience, kindness, leadership, organization, creativity, thoughtfulness, candor, hard-work, communication, etc., as well as the hard skills like writing, presenting, cooking, computer design and many many more.

Capacity is closely linked to ability. Think of capacity as the container and ability as liquid that fills it. The greater the capacity, the more opportunity there is for ability to be poured inside.

Here are some common types of abilities:

- Domain knowledge: Specific knowledge pertaining to a subject, industry, profession, or culture.

- Tacit knowledge: Skill that can only be gained through much practice or experience, such as playing football, or being an entrepreneur.

- Learning: The ability to absorb and memorize new information and apply it to your everyday life.

- Research: The process of discovering new information and assessing various knowledge sources.

- Problem-solving: Examining issues to identify the root cause and develop appropriate solutions.

- Emotional intelligence: The ability to read other people's emotions so you can navigate different social situations and adjust how you communicate with different types of people.

- Creativity: Brainstorming novel ideas that break away from conventional wisdom and finding new ways of solving problems or doing things.

- Strategy: Formulating plans to solve specific problems or achieve specific goals.

Talent vs. Skill

It's common for people to confuse talents for skills, and vice versa, even though they describe two different abilities. Talents, for instance, are natural abilities that you are born with, whereas skills are abilities you develop with time and experience. Talents can be fostered and improved with practice and appropriate guidance, but skills can only be gained through sheer hard work and determination.

A person born with a talent of public speaking can woo any crowd without having to do much preparation beforehand. They are naturally social, and with practice, they are able to develop emotional intelligence (a skill that enhances their natural talent of public speaking). This is different from a person who has to go to school to learn the art of public speaking and work hard to develop a sociable character. In the end, their ability to engage in public speaking is a result of a learned skill, not a natural talent.

Each individual has a set of natural and learned abilities. We cannot say that leveraging talents is better than leveraging skills, or that it is better to be an expert on a matter than to have a natural affinity for it. The value of talents and skills is determined by how each individual uses what they were born with, as well as what they have learned to live their Ikigai.

While it is easy to determine what you are skilled at because you have a physical track record, it can be difficult to identify your natural talents. You might erroneously pass off your talents as a character trait, like being a good conversationalist. You may also be inclined to reject your natural talents, particularly if you grew up in a household or community where your unique talents were seen as undesirable. Here are three processes you can practice to identify your natural talents so you can use them when living your Ikigai:

1. Reflection

For many it's typically easier to identify the gifts that others display than recognizing your own gifts. Let's face it—when it comes to acknowledging our own strengths, we can be quite critical! However, it's important for you to understand that just like anybody else, you were born with natural abilities to do things. There isn't a subgroup of humans with supernatural abilities that roam the world. Each and everyone of us, regardless of where we might come from or how we might be different, are born with talents.

Once you have accepted this truth about yourself, you will find less resistance in actually thinking about some of the abilities that come naturally to you. You don't have to think hard since these abilities occur effortlessly anyway. All you would need to do is revisit some memories of past experiences when you excelled without putting in much time or effort, or when others came to you for assistance related to that particular ability.

You can even reflect on the activities you flourished in during your teenage years. Or the kinds of praise or compliments you have heard over the course of your life from different people. You can even reflect on some of your best skills and identify patterns or themes that might point toward certain talents. For example, if you have a vivid imagination and are good at telling stories, you may have a natural talent for writing, poetry, or filmmaking.

Document your talents in a brainstorming session by writing down what comes to your mind on a piece of paper. Write as much as you can. It may be helpful to set a timer and brainstorm for a fixed amount of time, say 5 minutes. Just get these ideas out as fast and extensively as possible. And don't evaluate (or judge) your ideas. Not yet. We'll do that a bit in the next phase, Assessment.

2. Assessment

You now have a bunch of ideas of what could be potential talents. It's time to look at them more deeply. Go through each item on your list. Dig in. Drill down to the core of your talents. Are there core talents that underlie what you already have on the page? Are their sister talents that are in some way related or otherwise connected? Can you go more broad and identify bigger or more general concepts?

Rate your strength in each of these talents. Use

71

whatever system works for you. It could be 1-5 stars, happy-super happy faces, rookie-superstar, whatever. Just be realistic. Be honest. Don't overrate or underrate yourself.

In addition to this, taking a formalized assessment will give you the confirmation you need. There are many online talent assessments that are free and produce trusted results. The two that I recommend are the Myers-Briggs Type Indicator (MBTI) and the Clifton Strengths test. The MBTI is free and it can help you understand your personality type, which would give you a good indication of where your natural talents and strengths lie. The Clifton Strengths test is a paid online assessment that helps you find your talents using 177 paired statements. As useful as these assessments can be, keep in mind that they are only tools meant to help you make sense of different aspects of who you are. They can point you in the direction toward finding your talents and confirm strong inclinations that you already have.

3. Grounding

At this point, you should have a sheet of paper where you have written down what could be potential talents and results from your completed assessments of your talents and personality type. Now you can look at all of the information you have gathered and look for recurring ideas or patterns that point to your natural talents. In other words, based on the feedback or experiences you had growing up and the results from your assessments, what can you confidently say you are talented at? When you have confirmed what your natural talents are, you can do your research on each talent and explore the many ways it can be utilized or how it can be developed.

Strategies for Becoming a Master at Anything

When developing your abilities, you can practice the principle of Kodawari. Remember that Kodawari is the pursuit of excellence through actions. Thus, when learning a new skill or developing your natural talents, you can use Kodawari to reach the level of mastery. Kodawari is about the journey toward mastery, not the destination. It can lead you on the path of continual progress, learning, and growth. Below are five strategies that can help you apply Kodawari when seeking to master a skill or talent:

1. Don't Fear Discomfort

When pursuing anything outside of your comfort zone, be prepared for the shock or panic it brings in your body. Anything outside of the parameters of what you define as normal will feel frightening and to some extent dangerous. Since you have never set out to accomplish these goals before, you don't have an idea of what to expect. The feeling of discomfort is normal when venturing into the unknown. It is a sign that you are doing something courageous and pushing your own limits. This is the kind of environment necessary for growth and personal development, so embrace the fear, mistakes, or difficulties that you may face. Remember you don't need to make leaps and bounds outside your comfort zone today. Just push the edges a little. And little by little those edges will become more malleable and expand in time.

2. Avoid Over-Analyzing Your Plans

While it's good to plan and carefully consider what you intend to do, it's important not to get caught in analysis paralysis. There comes a point during the planning stage where you start overthinking your decisions to the extent of becoming overwhelmed and discouraged. There's only so much you can anticipate before you take the first step. As you continue to make progress, you will be able to adjust your plans according to your situations. Masters are strategic planners, but they are also risk-takers. They understand that actions speak louder than words, so they are quick to make moves and get the momentum going.

This is also a strong argument for taking baby steps. With baby steps the risk is significantly lower, so the potential detriment from just jumping in is minimal.

3. Find the Sweet Spot

According to Daniel Coyle, author of the book titled *The Talent Code*, you should aim to be successful 60% to 80% of the time while developing your skills or talents (The Week Staff, 2015). That is the sweet spot that helps you make significant improvement. It gives you enough of a challenge to stay committed while also making allowances for bad days, mistakes, and other unexpected obstacles along the way. When you find your sweet spot, you're able to maintain your progress in the long-term too. Your goals aren't too hard or too easy for you to achieve, which makes them appropriate to continue in the long run.

4. Study a Master

To master anything, you need to study the life of a real master who has achieved what you hope to one day achieve. A master can be anyone (including family, friends, or colleagues) who you believe has achieved some level of success in one particular area. There's no need to take on every challenge alone and there is so much to be learned from those who have the relevant expertise or experience. In this new era of the internet, it has become easier to find masters, gurus, and moguls online by going on sites like YouTube, LinkedIn, Instagram and so on. You can gain access to a successful person's life without even knowing them by simply watching their videos or listening to their podcasts. If you have the privilege of connecting with masters in person, then take full advantage of that. Nothing can beat sitting down with a master one-on-one and listening to them speak about their experience and give you valuable advice for your journey.

5. Keep a Notebook

Many successful artists, entrepreneurs, and inventors keep notebooks where they can document their ideas, thought processes, and experiences. Writing your thoughts in a notebook can help you reduce stress, sharpen your memory, improve your self-awareness, and encourage you to achieve your goals. If you want to improve upon your skills and talents, you will need to keep a record of your successes, challenges and gained insights so you can improve. You will need to document your highs and lows, what is working well, and what isn't, as well as the psychological impact of your journey. Make journaling a habit by dedicating a few minutes a day to sit with a notebook and reflect on your daily progress and anything else that may be weighing heavily on your mind.

What Is Community?

Community refers to your group. This can be the group of people who live in the same place, interact together or share similar values, beliefs, or interests. In essence, your family, circle of friends, neighborhood, company, industry association or social media group can be your community. Even though these groups may be structured differently, they are made up of people who share something and are connected in some way.

People need to be a part of a community to feel a sense of fulfillment in their lives. When you join a community, you can fulfill your need for belonging. The need for belonging refers to the need to connect with and be accepted by others. When a person spends too much time in isolation from others, they can experience psychological distress. Since humans are naturally social creatures, the inability to connect with others can feel threatening. Of course, the amount of connection each individual requires will differ, but maintaining meaningful relationships is something that everyone can benefit from.

If you break down the word community into the root and the suffix, you will get two words: common unity. This is the crux of a community—coming together to unite for common goals, beliefs, and interests. It can also describe coming together for protection against hardship and offering each other comfort amidst difficult times. When you are part of a community, your aim is to grow alongside other people and offer support as much as you are given support. Like any other relationship, members of a community practice reciprocation, striking a good balance between giving and taking. The balance between give and take is what ensures that every member's needs are met and that the community continues to thrive.

Being a part of a community can enhance your Ikigai because you commit to something bigger than yourself and work toward a common vision that can improve not only your life, but the lives of others. When you are a member of a community, you feel a sense of purpose in striving toward the highest possible good for the entire group, such as your family, neighborhood, district, nation, or world. Your purpose can be localized, like feeding homeless people in your area, or it can be broad, like doing your part to end global food waste.

Extend Your Value to Others

The reward of being a part of a community is having people who we can lean on for support as we go through our life's journey. However, it can also be rewarding to give back to our community and find ways of sharing our skills, knowledge, and experience with others. What's interesting is that as value is generously extended to others, a deep personal sense of fulfillment develops. This positive energy and good feeling is the reward for being useful to another person and helping them achieve their Ikigai too. Here are three tips to remember when extending your value to others:

1. Be Courageous

To add value to another person or organization, you will need to be courageous enough to step out and acknowledge your own value you have to offer. It may require the confidence to make the initial contact or take the first step in reaching out to another person and sharing your skills, knowledge, or talents with them. In a personal context, this could mean being courageous to offer a friend advice on a matter you have experience in, and in a professional context it could mean being courageous to propose a new idea that can benefit the organization or offer your assistance to a colleague that looks overwhelmed. It only takes 20 seconds of ridiculous courage to put yourself out there and potentially have an impact that lasts a lifetime.

2. Share Your Knowledge

It's possible to take for granted the amount of knowledge you hold. This is especially true when you are surrounded by other knowledgeable people who may know as much as you do and therefore seemingly don't have any need for your expertise. But the reality is that what you know can be valuable to those who desire to achieve what you have been able to achieve. You can broaden your community by finding people to mentor or share your knowledge with.

3. Continue to Work on Yourself

You can't be of value to others when you can't see the value in yourself. In order to share your skills, talents, and knowledge, you must first be confident in who you are and see your abilities as being worthwhile. How you look at yourself matters because it can be what empowers or blocks you from extending yourself to others. Work on identifying your strengths and weaknesses and finding your passions and abilities, so you can add value in everything you do for others.

Fear & the Barriers to Living Your Ikigai

We have looked at the three drivers of Ikigai, which are passion, capacity, and community. Building knowledge and improving each driver can make it easier for you to align to your purpose and maintain a purposeful life in the long-term. But despite your effort to find your passion, develop your abilities, and connect with those around you, you can be confronted with unique challenges that limit you from freely living your Ikigai. While there are a plethora of obstacles that can get in the way of living your Ikigai, the greatest of these is fear, particularly the fears of failure or success.

The Fear of Failure

Fear can be paralyzing. It can make the very opportunities you have been longing for feel intimidating or wrong. The fear of failure can leave you feeling stuck in routines that don't bring any joy or meaning to your life, only because you are afraid of failing at something which you deeply desire.

The fear of failure, like most fears, is rooted in subconscious beliefs that you have about yourself and your ability to succeed in life. For example, if you believe that you need to be perfect in order to receive love, you may enter a relationship having too high expectations for yourself and your partner. You may even attempt to control how the relationship progresses or struggle to be yourself. Your own imposed expectations can block you from receiving or giving love in return, which could end up sabotaging your relationship.

The fear of failure can manifest in different ways. Here are some common symptoms you can look out for:

- Being fearful of trying new experiences or voluntarily taking on new challenges.

- Displaying self-sabotaging behaviors, such as procrastinating, thinking negatively about your plans, or the inability to follow through with your goals.

- Having a low self-esteem and speaking poorly about yourself and your ability to succeed. You might say phrases like "I don't deserve that," or "I'm not strong enough to overcome this."

- Displaying perfectionist behaviors (which could be another form of self-sabotage), like having unrealistic expectations or standards and reacting negatively to constructive feedback or unexpected challenges.

The fear of failure makes everything beyond your control seem dangerous. When you succumb to this kind of fear, you may live a very rigid life with little to no progress. The reality is you can't escape failure. You are bound to fail at things that you haven't yet mastered. In other words, there is an enormous amount of risk that comes with growth and learning, but does that mean you shouldn't pursue growth and learning? Ideally, failure shouldn't be a barrier that makes you delay or abandon your plans. You should see it as feedback from the universe that your plans need to be adjusted or reworked. Failure should be a pitstop that you visit each time your plans need some more work, not a permanent place where you park and never move from.

The Fear of Success

The other side of the fear of failure is the fear of success. It seems rather strange that someone would fear a positive outcome, but the fear of success is more complicated than that. When an individual fears success they aren't necessarily afraid of accumulating wealth or landing their dream job. Instead, they fear the changes that will come as a result of achieving success, like how their personal character or relationships will change. Their subconscious beliefs related to success are what cause them to create fictional scenarios that make success seem undesirable. For example, a person may want to achieve financial stability, but the thought of making more money could cause them to abandon their goal. Why? Because they may have grown up believing that money is the root of all evil—a negative money belief that causes them to turn down money-making opportunities.

The fear of success can lead a person to sabotage their own efforts at succeeding at life. It's not that they don't believe in themselves enough or that they don't have the skills or talents to succeed. It's more about their fear of being exposed to negative outcomes that come with success. Here are a few examples that you can probably relate to:

- You want to become more confident speaking with different people but you are afraid of receiving "too much" attention from others or being in the spotlight.

- You want to be an expert in your field but fear that it may isolate you from your peers.

- You have always dreamed of owning a property but you fear what others might say about your expensive purchase.

- You desire to live an unconventional lifestyle but fear being judged or undermined because of it.

- You have always wanted to become a successful person but you worry that it could change your personality for the worse.

- You want to make more money but at the back of your mind you fear becoming materialistic.

- You would like to make a change in activities or lifestyle but avoid it because it would mean disconnecting in some way from your family, friends or community.

Both the fear of failure and the fear of success can sabotage your efforts at achieving your goals and living the quality of life you have always desired. Both fears can make the idea of reaching your full potential seem dangerous or not appropriate for you.

To overcome the fear of failure and success, consider what exactly you are afraid of. For instance, what is it about being rejected or actually getting accepted that makes you feel anxious? Is it the judgment you believe you will receive from others? Or the way in which success can inflate your ego? Then play the "what if" game. Ask yourself what if your fears actually come true. What would change? What would happen to you and how would you recover?

Thinking about the worst case scenario can help you manage your fears and come up with various coping strategies. If you do end up getting an ego boost, you could find ways to ground yourself by helping others or practicing gratitude. Lastly, you can remind yourself to focus on the process, not the destination. Pay attention to every small task in your grand plan and don't preoccupy yourself with the bigger picture. If you invest time and energy in mastering the small things, the big things will take care of themselves.

Chapter Takeaways

- Instead of thinking of your passions as fun pastime activities, start looking at them as meaningful pursuits that can take on a greater purpose in your life.

- What you are passionate about can also be linked to your natural talents or acquired skills. Don't discount your past life experiences—they can give you clues about the unique abilities you possess!

- Mastering anything requires considerable patience and a dedication to excellence. But this isn't something you should fear. Think big but work small and be intentional with every decision you make about your life.

- Expect discomfort and anxious thoughts when venturing into something new. This is a sign that you are being courageous and embracing the risk that comes with growth and learning. Don't get stuck in analysis paralysis or obsess about what other people will think or say. Remind yourself about what living in Ikigai means for you and take action!

You have successfully completed part one of the book. So far, you have learned about the origins and meaning of Ikigai, as well as some of the misconceptions about the philosophy. You have also learned the three drivers of Ikigai, how to use them to find your purpose, and the most common fear that can stand in your way. You are now ready to move on to part two of the book where we will focus on your personal development and how you can identify your value.

Part 2:

Finding Your Ikigai

Chapter 4:

Knowing Yourself, Knowing Your Ikigai

If something is illuminating you from the inside, you are meant to build an ultra legacy around it which will supersede your world.

— Hiral Nagda

What do you want to be remembered for?

In this chapter you will learn:

- The importance of knowing who you are when finding your Ikigai.

- How to take the Ikigai Assessment quiz.

- Rewriting your life story and taking control of your narrative!

The Necessity of Understanding Who You Are

What does it mean to know who you are? Is it about understanding your strengths and weaknesses, or does it go deeper than that? Aristotle said knowing who you are is the beginning of wisdom (Huebner, n.d.) What did he mean by this? When you know yourself you can lead your life more effectively and achieve the goals you set out for yourself. Knowing who you are helps you refine your character, get rid of ideas or beliefs that aren't aligned with your values or purpose, and create a lifestyle that you enjoy living.

Here are a few reasons why understanding who you are is so important:

- When you are able to articulate who you are, you will gain confidence and have a better chance of getting exactly what you want.

- You will feel less internal conflict because your words, behaviors, and attitudes will match the vision you have for your life.

- Knowing yourself helps you make informed decisions about your life and more easily navigate unexpected challenges.

- You will have better self-discipline because you understand the impact of your decisions and therefore won't deliberately sabotage your plans or progress.

- When you know yourself, you are more resistant to peer pressure and have better emotional regulation skills. When you receive criticism or judgment from others, you won't immediately react or take their words personally. Your beliefs about who you are carry a much greater weight than the opinions of others.

- You will be more tolerant and understanding of others because you have accepted your own weaknesses and can empathize with another person's suffering.

Meg Selig, the author of *Changepower! 37 Secrets to Habit Change Success*, shares the components that make up a person. These components can be seen as the building blocks of creating an identity. There are six components that form the acronym VITALS, which is short for values, interests, temperament, around-the-clock activities, life mission and goals, and strengths and skills. Below is an explanation of each component:

1. Values

Values are the beliefs and principles in life that you consider to be important. Your values inform your decisions, perspective about certain aspects of your life, such as family, and the kind of goals you set for yourself. Research has shown that by simply writing down what you value, you are more likely to think about it when taking action. Knowing what you value can also help you decide which areas of your life to prioritize. For example, if you value education, you may spend more time upskilling yourself than a person who doesn't share the same value.

2. Interests

Your interests can include your passions, hobbies, and anything that you are naturally drawn to. Take a moment and think about what subject or activity you are curious about, or invest a lot of your time on (this doesn't include your day job or any family obligations). Now think about the social causes you care about or that fascinate you. Your attention naturally gravitates toward the things that energize you and make you feel good. As you grow and learn, it is normal for your interests to change. What you are interested in depends on where you are in your life and what you have been exposed to. Therefore, gaining more life experience and exposure can broaden your interests.

3. Temperament

Temperament describes your human nature, like whether you are an introvert or extrovert, impulsive, or easy-going. In essence, it includes your natural human instincts that you resort to when you are simply living your life. Understanding your temperament is useful because it can help you navigate relationships, choose work that is suitable for you, and avoid chasing after goals that are not aligned to who you are and how you normally behave. Since each person has their own unique temperament, it is rare for people to react to life circumstances in the same way. By understanding your temperament, you can face challenges according to your unique temperament, rather than taking someone else's advice or modeling another person's behavior.

4. Around-the-Clock Activities

Around-the-clock activities refer to the time in which you prefer to do certain things. There are some people who are more focused when working at night and others who prefer to get work done early in the morning. Knowing which times of the day you prefer to do certain tasks, like working, eating, sleeping, or practicing self-care can help you create a procrastination-proof daily schedule. It will also help you manage your time wisely and feel happy about how you spend every minute of each day.

5. Life Mission and Goals

What makes a meaningful life? Having a purpose that grounds you and helps you navigate through life more efficiently. A life mission is what you set out to do in your life. Once again, your mission can evolve as you grow and learn, but at each phase of your life, it becomes the driving force that keeps you determined to achieve your goals. Your goals are the aims that you set to help you accomplish your life mission. For example, if your life mission is to share happiness with others, your goals will be the various things you can do to achieve that, such as adopting an optimistic worldview or making gratitude a daily practice.

6. Strengths and Skills

Your strengths are normally the abilities you naturally possess. These may include your talents or character strengths, such as being trustworthy. Your skills on the other hand are abilities that you have learned over the years as a result of practice and learning. Having a good understanding of your strengths and skills can improve your self-confidence. Not only do you believe you are valuable, you have sufficient proof of it too! You learn to accept that you have something to offer the world, just like anybody else, and leverage what you have been given to move ahead in your life.

The VITAL components of who you are can help you learn how to be yourself. While being yourself is easier said than done, making an effort to determine who you are and what makes you different can make you less likely to conform to societal ideals. You are unique—but you can't rely on anyone else to tell you that. You need to discover your uniqueness on your own so that you can present yourself as a secure and confident individual who is in control of their life.

Ikigai and Finding Yourself

There is no greater pursuit in life than the pursuit of finding yourself. In our early years, we accept the projections others put on us as being who we are. This causes us to live our lives at the mercy of others or in constant search for external validation. However, in order for us to be productive and happy, we must find our own unique flow and live our lives according to it.

Some believe that self-discovery is a self-centered pursuit. This is not true. There is nothing self-centered about getting to know who you are, what your strengths are, and how you differ from others. While the focus is on you, the purpose is to become a better version of yourself so that you can live a meaningful life and make a positive contribution to those around you. Think of self-discovery as being a process where you shed layers that don't suitably align with your actual needs and goals, and reveal new layers that reflect the growth you have made, and can make, in your life.

What does this have to do with Ikigai? It's rare to just wake up one morning and suddenly know what your purpose is. It's a poor plan to hope to simply stumble onto your purpose as though it were a spontaneous butterfly that randomly landed on your nose. To find your Ikigai, or purpose, you must be willing to go on a journey of self-discovery and figure out who you are or who you desire to be. To embrace your Ikigai you must first find your personal power, which is the confidence to be yourself. This isn't something you ought to be afraid of. It's already within you. You are already powerful. The only thing left to do is activate your personal power.

Here are a few methods for introspection that can help you find your Ikigai:

1. Reflect On Your Past

Have you ever wondered why counselors will always start counseling sessions by asking you about your background or childhood upbringing? It is because the majority of your beliefs, behaviors, and attitudes stem from your early childhood experiences. It takes about seven years for your subconscious mind to fully develop. This means that the first seven years of your life have shaped your perception of who you are, your understanding of relationships, and your outlook on the world. And since this information was learned and stored in your subconscious mind, you were hardly aware of the impact of the positive or negative information you were believing to be true.

It is difficult to make sense of the person you are today without digging deep into your past and identifying patterns of behavior or belief systems that were a detriment to your understanding of who you are. For example, if you find it difficult to express your thoughts and emotions as an adult, you might find that this problem stems from the relationship you had with your parents when you were younger. Reflecting on your past can prove that some of the tendencies you believe are part of your personality, are simply coping strategies or trauma responses you adopted as a child.

2. Differentiate

In psychology, differentiation is the ability to see yourself as an individual, having separate needs and goals than others. Children raised in dysfunctional home environments tend to grow up without the knowledge or confidence to set healthy boundaries. They might have had extremely controlling or manipulative parents who didn't respect or acknowledge personal space, privacy, or boundaries. As adults, these individuals struggle to create boundaries with others and may even develop codependency or people-pleasing behaviors. In other words, they don't have the tools to create a separate self from others and protect their own interests. To live a free and empowered life, you need to feel as though you are in control of your destiny and that you have the ability to respond to your own needs. While it's never easy to say no or choose a different path from others, finding your Ikigai requires you to develop your own set of values, beliefs, and ideals.

3. Look for Meaning

Viktor E. Frankl was an Austrian psychiatrist, neurologist, and Holocaust survivor. While living in a Nazi concentration camp, he decided to find a sense of meaning that would help him endure the horrific circumstances he was in. One of his famous quotes says, "Between stimulus and response there is a space. In that space is our power to choose our response. In our response lies our growth and our freedom (Frankl, n.d.)" The response he refers to is the meaning you ascribe to a given situation or to the various life stages you may go through. Your survival and happiness in life depends on maintaining a sense of meaning, even in the worst kinds of circumstances. To do this, you must try to look at the bigger picture and find the significance in where you are in life and how your life is unfolding.

4. Believe in Your Personal Power

As mentioned above, your personal power is the confidence to be yourself. When you are confident in who you are, you have the conviction to take control of your life (this also means taking responsibility for your actions). Although circumstances may be outside your control, you realize that your life's "success" is dependent upon your approach. When you change your approach to life, your entire worldview can change as well. Where you once saw lack, you see opportunities for growth and you are able to turn hopeless situations around. You become the hero or heroine in your story. The entire narrative of your life changes. You can practice believing in your personal power by recognizing the role you play in bringing positive change in your life, shifting your outlook from being a victim to being the survivor or hero, and being proactive rather than submissive or passive when taking action.

5. Recognize the Inner Critic

You have the power to be your own biggest cheerleader or your own worst critic. Indeed, there is no one more judgmental or cynical than you when it comes to analyzing your own life, nor should there be. You have the most invested in it.

The inner critic is the metaphoric "devil" that sits on your shoulder and affirms negative beliefs you have about yourself. Destructive thoughts are liable to cause delays or sabotage your progress. When you recognize this negative voice in your mind, you are able to distinguish between your self-limiting beliefs and who you actually are. This way, you won't be held back by a negative belief because you understand that it isn't a true reflection of your character or capabilities.

Therefore, to find your Ikigai, you must first find yourself. This is a bonus you get when seeking your purpose. Finding yourself is by far the most pleasurable and interesting journey you will ever undergo. Even though it involves the challenge of unlearning unproductive behaviors and reframing your mindset, the final outcome is that you feel confident in who you are and gain the self-motivation to live your Ikigai.

Your Ikigai Assessment

Here is a short quiz that consists of a series of short questions to determine your current level of active Ikigai. The quiz is based on your knowledge of self, abilities, community needs, and engagement of activities that incorporate those three areas.

Your answers will be A, B or C. At the end, tally up the number of each answer and see which category you fall under. If your answers fall somewhere between two of the categories, note that as well and take it into consideration as you check the result categories.

1.   How well do you know what you wish to learn?

> A) Not at all. I don't know yet what I wish to learn.

> B) Very well. I'm clear on what I wish to learn.

> C) I have somewhat of an idea of what I wish to learn.

2. Is it a challenge to maintain motivation during the week?

A) Yes, it's hard to find things to look forward to.

B) No, I have several projects and/or various interests that keep me engaged throughout the week.

C) It depends.

3. Do your days start off on a positive beat?

A) No. My mornings are chaotic.

B) Yes. Mornings are no problem for me.

C) It's hit or miss. I have a morning ritual but don't practice it consistently.

4. How well do you live by your core values?

A) I sometimes forget about my core values.

B) I am intentional about living each day embracing at least one core value.

C) At home I am able to practice my core values, but at work or in social settings, not so much.

5. How often do you engage in activities you have great interest and/or are passionate

about?

> A) Hardly ever. I don't have the time and I am not active when I do have free time.

> B) Yes, I engage in several activities that I'm interested in and passionate about to pass the time.

> C) I've been looking into taking up something and I'm still considering what to do with my free time.

6. Are you a valued and vital member of your family, social group, community, etc.?

> A) No, I'm still finding my feet and working on myself.

> B) Yes, I take pride in the responsibilities I have at home, work, and in my community. It feels good to make a small contribution.

> C) I like the idea of contributing to my family, work, and community, but I still need to find the most meaningful role I could play.

7. You are comfortable and lose track of time

when you are at work or while pursuing your passion.

    A) No, not at all.

    B) Yes, and it feels amazing!

    C) Somewhat.

8. Do you have a solid support network?

    A) No, I haven't found like-minded people or people who accept me as I am.

    B) Yes, my support network is broad and consists of different kinds of people who add value to my life.

    C) I don't know about "solid" but I do have a few people I can reach out to for support.

9. Do you have a significant relationship with someone (family, friend, significant other) with whom you are comfortable expressing yourself and sharing your feelings?

    A) Actually, I feel uncomfortable with intimacy.

    B) Yes, I do.

C) I have a few relationships but they aren't fulfilling/healthy.

10. Is there a particular quality, skill, or talent that you excel at?

A) I still need to discover my own unique qualities, skills, and talents.

B) Yes, I am known for at least one quality, skill, or talent.

C) Not that I am aware of.

11. Do you enjoy simple pleasures from time to time?

A) There's too much to worry about for that.

B) Yes. It's the small things that make life worth living.

C) I try to, but it's a challenge.

Assessment Results

Mostly A's: Self-Inquiry Stage

If you have answered mostly A's, you are at the beginning stages of self-inquiry. You may have identified a few personal challenges that are keeping you from living a wholesome and fulfilling life. At this stage, your main goal should be to continue exploring aspects of who you are and stepping out of your comfort zone. Yes, exploring the unknown can feel uncomfortable, but your growth lies beyond your current routines and lifestyle choices. Make it your mission to try new experiences, learn new skills, and adopt healthy behaviors and habits that can support the quality of life you desire.

Mostly B's: Active Ikigai Stage

If you have answered mostly B's, you are actively living your Ikigai. You have gone through the self-inquiry stage and have a firm understanding of who you are and what you desire in your life. You likely have healthy boundaries with others but can still be open and vulnerable when necessary. Your life is full of several meaningful pursuits; some big projects and other small rituals that keep you mentally and emotionally strong. Your vision for your life is clear and you have a good network of people who play their unique roles in helping you achieve success in life. You have a growth mindset and see learning as a continuous process that leads to mastery.

Mostly C's: Transformation Anxiety Stage

If you have answered mostly C's, you have somewhat embraced your Ikigai but still go back and forth in your mind about whether you are ready for the change. Unlike people in the self-inquiry stage, you are aware of who you are and what you desire in your life, but you fear the outcomes of your personal transformation. You have a tendency to resort back to old habits and behaviors or give up on yourself when you are getting close to your breakthrough. Your main goal at this stage is to work on building your personal power and challenging your negative self-beliefs. The only way you can succeed in life is if you believe that you can and that you deserve success. Surround yourself with people who are confident, secure, and are actively pursuing their goals so you can have positive influences that inspire you to continue seeking your Ikigai.

Exercise to Find Your Ikigai

With a little bit of introspection and brainstorming, you can find your Ikigai. This exercise requires you to have a pen and notebook. Below are four stages that you must complete to determine your Ikigai. The four stages include: Brainstorming, analyzing and identifying patterns, visualization, and taking action. Here is an outline of each stage and how you can complete the exercise:

Stage 1: Brainstorming

Write down words, themes, or ideas that come to your mind when you think about your passions, capacity and community. What you write down doesn't have to make sense at this point; your focus should be on getting as many thoughts on the pieces of paper as possible. Think of the things that set your heart on fire and make your living worthwhile. These could include activities you are already engaged in or activities you desire to one day fulfill. Then consider the various talents and skills that have shaped you into the person you are today. These could also be talents and skills that still need to be developed. Lastly, brainstorm some of the community needs you have observed that you could assist with. For instance, how can you make a positive difference to your home life? School? Workplace? Or neighborhood? When thinking about your impact make sure your contribution is something you can give or share that comes naturally or easily for you.

Stage 2: Analyze and Identify Patterns

From the notes you have written, look for recurring themes or ideas that come up. Observe the general behaviors or activities that appear more than once. If your ideas indicate an affinity for a particular talent or skill, write this down. For example, if you find that you have love to express your thoughts and socialize with people you may have an affinity for public speaking. Remember that a pattern only forms when there is a sufficient amount of evidence to create a trend. Write down all of the trends you can identify from your brainstorming notes and prepare for stage 3.

Stage 3: Visualize

This stage requires you to activate your creative brain. Take a few moments to analyze the trends that you have identified, and when you are ready close your eyes. With these trends at the forefront of your mind, pick one trend to focus on at a time and envision how it would play out in real life. For example, if you identified a trend of encouraging people to get through tough times, you can envision how this would play out if it were a central theme in your life. How would your life positively change if you spent each day finding ways to encourage people? How would this impact your family, work, or community? And how would you feel about yourself or your life? If you had to imagine your ideal day with this particular trend as the central theme, how would your day start and progress?

Stage 4: Take Action

At this point, you have identified a few trends that have appeared throughout your life and point to your Ikigai. However, the only way you can know for sure if you have truly found your Ikigai is to take action and start taking these trends seriously. You can find ways of turning your passions into hobbies or expressing your positive qualities at work. You can also make adjustments to your daily routine so that you have time to develop certain strong talents and skills. You will need to have a detailed plan to help you pursue your Ikigai. More on how to do this in the following chapter!

Your Ikigai—Past, Present, and Future

If your Ikigai has always been a part of you, it means that even before you became aware of who you are or that you needed to make positive changes in your life, there was a purpose you had to live out in your life. Those previous years where you felt like you were stuck or down in the dumps had a purpose to serve in your life. It probably didn't feel like there was any light to be found in those past experiences, but there was!

You see, Ikigai is not always something one would associate with pleasure. There are seasons where your Ikigai is to endure suffering and come out stronger on the other side. While this may not feel pleasurable, it still adds meaning to your life and causes you to become a resilient person.

There was once a successful farmer who had grown crops for many years. One day, his horse ran away and his neighbors came to comfort him. "That was so unfortunate," they said.

"Maybe," the farmer responded.

A few days later, the neighbors saw the farmer's horse approaching from a distance, running with three other wild horses. They exclaimed: "You are so lucky to have your horse return plus three more horses to help you on the farm!"

"Maybe," the farmer responded.

One day, the farmer's son was riding one of the wild horses when he got kicked off and broke his leg. "What a pity," the neighbor said sympathetically.

"Maybe," the farmer responded.

While his son was still nursing his broken leg, the military went door-to-door in the small village, recruiting young boys to join the army. When they arrived at the farmer's house, they saw a young boy with a broken leg and turned away. The neighbors praised the farmer for how well things turned out for him, but again he responded: "Maybe."

This Zen story shows the kind of attitude you can choose to have about life. Whether you are doing well or doing badly, you cannot see an event as being final. Throughout your life, you have been tested in many different ways through the various challenges you have overcome. Even though some of these challenges brought about pain, they were instrumental in carrying out your Ikigai.

Take a moment to reflect on your past, present, and future. Starting with your past, what would you say was your Ikigai about 5-10 years ago? Think of a few significant memories or milestones that can help you identify what your Ikigai was at the time. When you are ready, you can think about your Ikigai in the present moment—what is your purpose in this phase of your life? And before you lose your train of thought, jump ahead to the future and consider what you would like your Ikigai to be. Your life is constantly in motion and whether you are aware of it or not, each moment is incredibly meaningful!

Life Crafting to Live Your Best Life

Have you ever thought to yourself: "What is the plan for my life?" Maybe this thought came to you during a life transition where you were forced to embrace change. Or after realizing that time is passing and you still haven't figured out your life mission. Answering this kind of question isn't easy. After all, none of us really have our lives completely figured out. However, if we do manage to wrap our minds around the question, we can start the process of self-inquiry.

Life crafting is a tool that you can use when attempting to answer the question—What is the plan for my life? By reflecting on different aspects of your life across time, you can clarify your life purpose, develop meaningful goals, and feel grounded in who you are. Life crafting can be beneficial if you need some guidance in modifying your life story. Everybody has a life story, but not everyone is in control of their own narrative. There could be external forces, people, and ideals that seek to control how you live your life or how you define your purpose. When you succumb to the influences of these external forces, people, or ideals you can feel stuck, lost, or hopeless.

Here are a few more consequences of not controlling your own narrative:

- **You focus more on one aspect of your life and neglect the others.** If you are living in a major city where career advancement is equated to success, you might invest a significant amount of your time on establishing yourself career-wise and neglect other important aspects of your life, such as your health, hobbies, family, or other passions.

- **You end up living someone else's dream, not your own.** If you grew up with overbearing parents who desired to live vicariously through you, they may have persuaded you to define your purpose around the desires that mattered most to them—not you. At the end, you are able to fulfill their longings, but feel unsatisfied because you aren't able to pursue your own desires.

- **You find ways to numb yourself to your reality.** If you aren't in control of your own narrative, you won't enjoy living your life. This could lead to you adopting harmful coping behaviors like excessive drinking, smoking or other negative behaviors so you can numb yourself to the reality of your life. You may also be excessively dependent on others for support, affection, and guidance, which may lead to toxic relationship dynamics like codependency.

- **You conform to the norms and beliefs of modern society.** Modern society often doesn't support individualism. It has been set up to encourage collective ideas and beliefs, which isolates the unique perspectives and desires of individuals. Modern society trains you that it's selfish to think about yourself because you should be thinking about others. It tells you that you need to aim for the common good of all people, making your definition of "good" seem unprogressive or undesirable.

After practicing life crafting, you will be able to better understand your personal "why," like why you are still alive, why you were born with certain characteristics, and why you had to experience the events you did in the past. This will enable you to create your own sense of direction, without being influenced by what anyone else thinks. Life crafting doesn't only involve planning out your life; it also involves envisioning your goals, reflecting on the things that make you sad or happy, and the beliefs you stand for.

An important part of life crafting is writing about life experiences, values, passions, and future aspirations. By writing down your thoughts and feelings you get to clarify your intentions and map out your life, using your own words and ideas. To do life crafting appropriately you need to give yourself at least 15 minutes to write about your life. If you can't find 15 minutes in your day, schedule a slot in advance. It's important not to feel rushed when thinking about your various life experiences. When you are calm and engaged, you will find it easier to tap into your subconscious mind and access deep thoughts and feelings.

Here is a simple life crafting activity that you can practice at home to begin rewriting your life story:

In a notebook, write about the following aspects of your life (there are no wrong or right answers):

1. Values and Passion

- What you enjoy doing.

- What kind of intimate relationships you would like to have.

- What kind of professional relationships you would like to have.

- Healthy lifestyle choices you would like to embrace.

2. Current and Desired Competencies

- The qualities you admire in other people.

- The qualities you admire in yourself.

- Your own habits that you like and dislike.

- Desired skills you would like to learn.

3. Current and Future Social Life

- Current relationships that energize you.

- Current relationships that discourage you.

- Qualities that you admire in friends.

- Kind of friendships you desire to have in the future.

- What your ideal family life looks like.

Chapter Takeaways

- When you have a good understanding of who you are, you won't be easily led astray by other people's desires or opinions of your life.

- Knowing yourself helps you build your personal power, which is the confidence you have in being yourself.

- Every phase of your life has its purpose, even if the experience isn't pleasurable. Even in horrific circumstances, there is still meaning to be drawn from your experience.

- If you desire a sense of direction in life, you can practice life crafting by reflecting on various life experiences and how they have shaped you into the person that you are, and given you the courage to take charge of your future.

You are the most valuable asset in your life. Investing in yourself is what will help you live a meaningful existence. Now that you are pumped to take charge of your life story, it's time we discussed strategies for taking action and implementing Ikigai in your life.

Part 3:

Living Your Ikigai

Chapter 5:

Make Intentional Decisions

Man does not simply exist but always decides what his existence will be, what he will become the next moment. By the same token, every human being has the freedom to change at any instant.

— — Victor E. Frankl

What will it take for you to start today?

In this chapter you will learn:

- What the 1% rule is about and how it can be applied to Ikigai.

- The five laws to implement the 1% rule in your everyday life.

- How developing your mental strength can help you quickly pick yourself up after facing a setback.

Ikigai and the 1% Rule

In finance, there is a concept known as compound interest. It refers to the interest you earn on your investment that grows year by year. For example, if I invest $10 in a savings account and earn 10% interest each year, in five years my $10 would have grown to $16.45. The interest would have built on itself. It would have compounded. What does this have to do with implementing Ikigai in your life? Well, it's simple. Each intentional decision you make to reinforce the quality of life you desire will eventually add up and transform your entire life. In other words, small and consistent action taken over an extended period of time is enough to change how you live and experience your life. The concept of compound interest shows that it is the small adjustments you make to your life that end up yielding the greatest rewards. The improvements you make will build upon themselves. They will compound.

This tends to go against what we have been taught, which is to think and aim high. While it is important to have meaningful aspirations, when you get down to doing the work, you will need to focus on the smaller tasks or goals that help you get ahead. There are times when thinking big can be a distraction or make the journey toward your Ikigai seem too demanding. But when you shift your focus to what you can do on a daily basis to live a healthier and happier life, suddenly implementing Ikigai becomes much more doable.

The 1% rule suggests making 1% improvement on a daily basis to achieve your goals. From first glance, 1% improvement doesn't look like much at all. However, just like compound interest, small and consistent change done over time can bring an immense amount of transformation. Let's bring the subject back to your Ikigai for a moment. It can be intimidating setting out to live a purposeful life. Your Ikigai may even be so extraordinary that you are confused about where to begin. Practicing the 1% rule can help you ease into the new life you plan for yourself and continue making progress at a comfortable pace. Here are five ways the 1% rule can help you live your Ikigai:

1. **Making small improvements every day is sustainable.** Instead of flipping your whole life upside down, you can implement change on a micro level and slowly integrate the new habits, beliefs, and lifestyle choices you desire. Moreover, since 1% change requires very little effort, you are less likely to procrastinate when completing your daily goals.

2. **Each small milestone you achieve can boost your self-confidence.** When you count your many small wins, you will develop confidence in your ability to succeed. And when you believe in yourself, you are more likely to stay committed to your goals.

3. **You can track your progress on a daily or weekly basis.** The benefit of making small improvements is that you can assess your progress on a regular basis and make adjustments to your plans when necessary. You can also address challenges sooner rather than later, which helps to keep your momentum going!

4. **You get to focus on the details.** Remember the principle of Kodawari? The pursuit of excellence? What better way to practice this principle than to commit yourself to small tasks that you can improve on as time goes on. Making small adjustments to your lifestyle can help you zone in on the intricacies of each move you make so that you can achieve the quality of results you seek.

5. **Making small improvements helps you move at your own pace.** It can be tempting to

observe the life of a successful person and desire to implement the same strategies they used to achieve success. The truth is what worked for someone else may not work for you—even if the goals are the same. Making small changes on a regular basis helps you find your own rhythm and progress at your own pace. Instead of modeling someone else's journey, you customize your own.

6. **You can be agile.** Making micro-adjustments allows you to course correct with ease. Does your strategy need amending? Has new information come into play? No problem. Because you are implementing small changes you are more easily and readily able to realign your actions quickly and adapt with agility.

5 Laws for Practicing the 1% Rule

Author Tom O'Neil wrote the book titled, *The 1% Principle*, which is based on the 1% rule (O'Neil, 2013). In this book, he motivates readers to make small changes to reach big goals, such as losing weight or starting a new career. To help readers make 1% improvements every day, O'Neil presented eight laws to live by. Below are five of the laws which can help you make incremental changes in your life:

1. The Law of the Small

This law states that you shouldn't neglect the small things in life because they are what lead to change (whether positive or negative). For example, if you pay no attention to the quality of food you eat, you probably won't experience any significant short-term effects on your body (besides indigestion, fatigue, or gaining a bit of weight). However, in the long run, your poor diet can lead to chronic diseases, like diabetes or heart disease, which can be deadly. Therefore, by taking care of the minor tasks, habits, or thoughts, you can influence the bigger outcomes.

2. The Law of Cumulative Effect

Have you noticed how having a small negative thought can profoundly impact your mood? And once your mood is negative, you are more prone to utter negative words or act impulsively? This explains the Law of Cumulative Effect. Change in one area of your life is likely to influence change in another area of your life. Therefore, by paying attention to the kinds of choices you make, you can trigger a snowball effect and bring about positive change in various areas of your life. For example, the decision to wake up an hour earlier seems arbitrary. However, when you wake up an hour earlier you may have more time to properly prepare yourself for the day, which could impact your overall mood during the day and help you manage time more effectively.

3. The Law of Positive and Negative

This law states that a decision is either good or bad and it can either bring about good or bad outcomes in your life. In other words, your daily choices can help you get closer into achieving your goals or cause unnecessary delays or barriers. It's important to take time to think before making any decision concerning yourself or others. Avoid reacting to circumstances, especially when you are feeling emotional. Give yourself enough time to calm down, understand what exactly is happening, and weigh your options. Choose to respond in a way that will benefit those involved and understand that your response, your choice, has impact.

4. The Law of Decision and Action

One of the reasons people struggle to achieve their goals is because they delay in making decisions. Instead of weighing their options and taking the most beneficial course of action, many people over-analyze their options and get caught up in overthinking. Every decision has its risks—this is inescapable. To move forward in life, we need to accept the potential risks that come with our decisions and choose to proceed with them anyway. Nonetheless, what is more important than making a decision is actually following through with it until you have reached completion. Following through with your decision will help you learn from the process, refine your strategy, and avoid repeating the same errors.

5. The Law of the Paradox

This law states that to gain something tomorrow, you must be willing to give up something today. In other words, embracing change and transforming your life will require you to give up some of your old lifestyle choices, friendships, beliefs, and any other part of your past that can rob your future. Letting go of something you may have held onto for a number of years may be extraordinarily difficult, but remind yourself of the value of what you are currently chasing after. Finding and living your Ikigai will come at some cost and you may need to be willing to pay that price upfront before you can actually experience the reward of living in your purpose.

Ikigai for Facing Difficult Challenges

Have you ever come across people who always seem to bounce back from personal failures? I'm sure you wondered what it was about them that gave them the confidence to rise from the ashes. It is mental strength that enables people to overcome challenges and accept new ones. Mental strength is the capacity you have to manage the various stressors in your life and continue making progress despite setbacks.

You can think of mental strength as being a muscle that you need to constantly exercise to make it big and strong. A variety of mental tools and techniques can help you develop your mental strength, and finding your Ikigai is one of them. When you know who you are and what you want out of life, you achieve mental clarity and are able to focus on meaningful tasks and goals. When you experience a sudden setback, it doesn't derail you from your vision. All it means is that you need to find another route or strategy to achieve your milestone. Failure is less likely to make you quit on yourself or your goals because you have found purpose in how you live your life.

For example, you may desire to achieve an MBA because it will help you get ahead in your career. If you fail a module or a semester during the course of your studies, you are less likely to quit and forget about your goal. Why? Because there is a deeper underlying purpose for getting an MBA that keeps you going. Thus, instead of quitting the entire MBA program, you may extend your program, find a tutor, or invest more time in studying your books. In essence, you re-route and find another way of overcoming the challenge.

Developing mental strength requires a level of self-awareness, resilience, and commitment. For instance, without being aware of your strengths and weaknesses, you might be blindsided by failure and without the willingness to follow through with your goals until completion, you may struggle to pick yourself up after a setback. Ian Turner (2017) described the four C's for building mental strength, which included: Control, commitment, challenge, and confidence.

1. Control

To feel mentally strong and healthy, you must genuinely believe that you are in control of your life and sense of purpose. The more control you have over your life, the higher your self-esteem will be. You need a high self-esteem to make sense of difficult life situations without blaming or judging yourself. In other words, you are able to separate who you are from your current life circumstances. Having control is also about regulating your emotions and not being easily influenced by the thoughts and feelings of others. You are able to set boundaries in your relationships that protect you from taking on more responsibility than you can assume.

2. Commitment

Your commitment shows the extent to which you can be reliable for achieving your goals. When your commitment is high, you can take responsibility for your actions and work through difficult situations. When things don't go your way, you are less likely to abort your mission or pass blame onto others. Moreover, your commitment keeps you focused and consistent in achieving your goals and limits the number of distractions that can lead you astray. When you demonstrate both control and commitment, you become resilient. Resilience is what makes it easier for you to adapt to unfavorable circumstances and keep moving forward.

3. Challenge

Everyone needs a challenge in life because challenges are what drive growth and learning. Without feeling challenged, you won't feel encouraged to keep pursuing your goals. People who embrace challenges tend to be mentally stronger than those who hide away from challenges. They are not fearful of change and can quickly adapt to new experiences without feeling disorientated. They perceive challenges as opportunities, rather than threats, and having this kind of mindset helps them overcome difficult situations.

4. Confidence

True confidence is believing in your ability to succeed in life. To possess true confidence, you must first confront your self-limiting beliefs and change how you perceive yourself and your ability to succeed. Having self-confidence will motivate you to complete the tasks and goals you set for yourself and even aim to excel at what you do. You are more likely to embrace opportunities for change when you aren't intimidated by failure due to the amount of faith you have placed in yourself.

Consider the four C's outlines above. Reflect on the current actions you are taking in your life to keep going. Next, think about the ideal actions you should be taking to live a meaningful life. How can your ideal actions help you develop mental strength? How can they help you gain more control over your goals, emotions, and purpose? Lastly, think about the ways you can challenge yourself to maintain your ideal actions and stay committed until completion. Feel free to write down the ideas that come to mind while reflecting on these various questions.

Chapter Takeaways

- While it is good to think big when planning your life, the most meaningful actions are usually the small and consistent tasks you do every day.

- Making 1% improvement to your life on a daily basis doesn't seem like much, but similar to compound interest, the small improvements will multiply and lead to significant change.

- Finding your Ikigai won't eradicate suffering from your life, but it can improve your mental strength so that you are more resilient in the face of challenges.

There is no truer saying than this: "Actions speak louder than words!" While we are on the subject of taking action, let's explore how you can build resilience, set actionable goals, and adopt new habits that can help you live a meaningful life.

Chapter 6:

Think—Say (Write)—Do

Twenty years from now you will be more disappointed by the things that you didn't do than by the ones you did do. So throw off the bowlines. Sail away from the safe harbor. Catch the trade winds in your sails. Explore. Dream. Discover.

— H. Jackson Brown

What does your ideal day look like, and what small steps can you take to achieve it?

In this chapter you will learn:

- How to become more resilient in life so that you can weather any storm.

- The value of writing things down and how to prepare a personal mission statement.

- Strategies for taking action on your goals and living your Ikigai.

- Discussing the concept of Kaizen and how it can help you make small and continuous improvements in your life.

Think:

Improve Your Resilience

Being resilient is what helps you develop mental strength. Without resilience, you will find it difficult to commit to your plans and make your Ikigai sustainable. You can think of resilience as what keeps you committed to your purpose and mental strength as what keeps your inner fire burning. There are a number of ways to improve your resilience, such as cultivating self-discipline, developing a strong work ethic, setting specific and achievable goals, and strengthening your willpower. The key is to create your own custom plan that incorporates several strategies that will help you cultivate resilience.

Here are a few resilience-building strategies you can consider:

1. Learning Meaningful Skills

When you learn a new skill, you develop your competencies and level of mastery. When the skill is meaningful (has a specific purpose it serves in your life), it can enrich the way you live and navigate challenges. During difficult times, these meaningful skills will help you solve problems in the most efficient way possible.

They can also give you a confidence boost and make you feel more prepared to overcome challenges or embrace new opportunities.

2. Setting Meaningful Goals

Meaningful goals are aligned to your Ikigai and carry intrinsic value. You are more likely to remain resilient when pursuing meaningful goals because the reward is much greater than the obstacles or risks you may face while working toward them.

3. Making Meaningful Connections

During difficult times, the people within your support network can provide care, knowledge, or support to help you overcome your challenges. It's important to ensure that your connections are meaningful, meaning that you have healthy relationships with people who are invested in your personal development and are able to listen and support you.

4. Accept the Necessity of Change

Without change, you cannot achieve personal growth. Each phase that you go through in life has a valuable lesson that prepares you for the next phase. Therefore, it is for your own benefit that you embrace change because it is a sign of graduating to the next phase of your life. Acknowledge that you cannot continue living in your comfort zone if you desire to live a truly meaningful life.

5. Practice Self-Reflection

The reason self-reflection is so powerful is because it helps you put your life in perspective. You can make sense of past experiences, current challenges, and your future aspirations. Reflecting on your life can also make you feel grateful for where you are on your journey. You are thankful for the milestones you have accomplished and the ways you have grown as a person. When you focus on what you have, you realize that you have enough. There is nothing you lack because everything you will need to advance in life is already within you!

Self-reflective questions are key in giving you insight about where you are in life and what you need to work on to become more resilient. Here are a few self-reflective questions you can work through to review the progress you have made in your life so far:

- What are some of the major events that have been the most stressful in my life? How did I manage to cope with the stress? What coping strategies were most effective in helping me overcome these challenges?

- Who have been the most supportive people in my life? In what ways has each person played a valuable role in helping me overcome challenges?

- What have I learned about the way I handle fear? What are the common thoughts, behaviors, or beliefs I turn to whenever I am fearful?

- What keeps me feeling hopeful about the future? What do I tell myself to stay committed to my goals?

Say (Write):

Create a Personal Mission Statement

Dr. Gail Matthews, a psychology professor at the Dominican University in California, conducted a study about goal-setting with close to 270 participants. The results of the study revealed that people were more likely to achieve their goals if they wrote them down (Economy, 2018). The participants were divided into five groups. The first group was instructed to think about their goals but not write them down. At the end, this group achieved a 43% success rate on completing their goals.

140

The second, third, and fourth groups were instructed to think about and write down their goals. However, the third group was also told to write down their action commitments and the fourth group was told to write down their action commitments *and* share them with their close friends. The fifth group was instructed to take all of the steps taken by the other groups (thinking about goals, writing goals down, writing down action commitments, and sharing action commitments with close friends). As a result, the fifth group had by far the highest success rate on completing their goals, at 76%.

Writing your goals down on paper can help you get clear on what you want and how you plan on accomplishing it. It can help you structure your goals in a way that makes them achievable. Visualizing your goals is important, but you can't take action on thoughts. You need to physically write down your thoughts on paper to see whether they are practical and create a strategy to turn them into tangible things. Businessman and life coach, Grant Cardone, reportedly writes down his goals twice a day—in the morning and at night. He believes that doing this will help him keep his goals top of mind. He explains, "I want to wake up to it. I want to go to sleep and I want to dream about it...I want to write my goals down before I go to sleep at night because they are important to me, they are valuable to me and I get to wake up to them again tomorrow" (Economy, 2018).

Neuroscience can also explain the significance of writing down your goals. When the brain receives new information, it is sent to a region of the brain known as the hippocampus for the brain to analyze. The hippocampus will decide whether the information received is worth storing as short or long-term memory, or simply discarding. How does the brain choose between important and useless information? The greatest priority is given to information that is written down. Neuropsychologists call this the generation effect. For example, if you read a book about how to knit a scarf, you might remember some of the various techniques or methods you read. However, if you decide to re-write the techniques and methods, in your own words, after you have read through the book, you are more likely to remember most of what you wrote down.

So, what does writing things down have to do with your personal mission statement? Think about the value of a company mission statement. Before a company begins its operations, it will create a mission statement that defines who they are, the values they stand for, and the goals they hope to achieve. By creating a mission statement, the company is able to remain focused on what it desires to achieve without getting sidetracked. A personal mission statement serves a similar purpose in your life. It can help you define who you are, what you value, and keep you focused on the specific life goals you set out to achieve. Personal mission statements need to be written down in order for them to be memorable, as well as to make it easier for you to review your progress over time. You can refer to your personal mission statement on a regular basis to check how well you are living up to your values and making strides on your goals.

To inspire you and show you what a personal mission statement looks like, here are a few examples from some of the most successful people in the world (Forsey, 2021):

1. Maya Angelou (American poet and civil rights activist)

"My mission in life is not merely to survive, but to thrive; and to do so with some passion, some compassion, some humor, and some style."

2. Walt Disney (Founder of Walt Disney Production)

"To make people happy."

3. Oprah Winfrey (Founder of Oprah Winfrey

Network)

"To use my gifts of intelligence, charisma, and serial optimism to cultivate the self-worth and net-worth of women around the world."

4. Malala Yousafzai (Nobel Peace Prize winner and activist)

"I want to serve the people. And I want every girl, every child to be educated."

5. Amanda Steinberg (Financial expert and entrepreneur)

"To use my gifts of intelligence, charisma, and serial optimism to cultivate the self-worth and net-worth of women around the world."

If you would like to create your personal mission statement, you can follow these simple templates. Feel free to customize your personal mission statement anyway you want:

1. **To [what you want to do] by [how you will do it] so that [the potential impact you can make].**

Here is an example:

"To offer words of encouragement to young people by

creating relevant personal development books so they can be mentored through various stages of adolescence."

2. **I value [what you value] because [why it matters]. To do this, I will need to [what habits you can adopt to align with what you value].**

Here is an example:

"I value confidence because it helps me express who I am in the most authentic way. To do this, I will need to recite positive affirmations about myself each morning to help me develop confidence in myself.

3. **To use my [skills or talents] to inspire/lead/teach [a group of people] so that [ultimate impact you can make].**

Here is an example:

"To use my financial background to teach people who are financially illiterate how to manage their money better and get out of debt, so that more households can build and sustain wealth.

Do:

Take Action on Your Mission

Once you have created your personal mission statement, all that's left to do is to take action. Your actions are what brings your dreams to life. There's a difference between taking action and "going with the flow." Anyone can move in whatever direction their life is taking them. It doesn't require us much effort to wake up in the morning and continue performing the same old routines we have committed to for many years. But taking action is about choosing to do the right thing, even if it means going on a different life path or adopting new habits and attitudes.

For example, taking action isn't about working longer hours at work or filling up your schedule so that you are constantly engaged in different tasks. The real definition of taking action is engaging in activities or making decisions that will lead you where you desire to go. This means that if working longer hours at work won't yield the results you hope for, then it shouldn't be considered as taking action. However, if your goal is to develop your competencies or improve your chances of success in the company, then working longer hours at work could be considered as such.

Therefore, before you decide to take any action, ask yourself: Am I doing the *right thing*? Remember that the right thing for one person may not be the same for another. Determine what doing the right thing looks and feels like for you, then and only then take the necessary actions. When you are ready to take action, you can follow this simple step-by-step guide to ensure that your decisions are aligned with your Ikigai and personal mission statement:

1. Start By Setting SMART Goals

SMART goals are specific, measurable, achievable, relevant, and time-based. If your goals are not specific enough, you might not know where and how to start. Similarly, if they are too big or require resources that you don't already have, you cannot sustain them in the long-term. Furthermore, ensure that your goals are meaningful and are rooted in something you find valuable. Here are a few questions you can ask yourself to determine if your goals are meaningful:

- Can you articulate your goal in a single sentence?

- Why does this goal matter to you?

- What will achieving this goal do for you?

2. Map Out Your Action Plans

This step requires you to map out your goals so you can determine what steps you need to take. Start by writing down each goal and creating a chronological list of steps that it will take to achieve the goal. Keep the steps specific and simple so that you know exactly what you need to do and the resources you will need to carry out each step. You can also make each step small enough so that you are encouraged to take action immediately. To give you a clearer understanding of what your life might look like once your plans are in motion, you can also map out what your day will look like when you start taking the right action.

3. Avoid Procrastination By Scheduling Your Action Steps

If you want to be consistent in taking action, you need to schedule your goals in your calendar. Consider how much time you will need to carry out an action step and block out time in your calendar. Some action steps will need to be done on a daily basis and others can be done on a weekly or monthly basis. Be realistic about how much time you are able to put aside for completing your action steps. If you won't have time during the week, then block out time on the weekends.

4. Create "If/Then" Scenarios

As dedicated as you might be in achieving your goals,

there will be times when you experience unexpected challenges. To ensure that unexpected challenges don't hinder your progress, you need to plan ahead and decide what you will do when put in that position. Creating "If/then" scenarios can help you anticipate setbacks and determine the best course of action to take. For example, you can decide that if a certain problem arises, you will adopt a certain coping strategy or make a certain decision. An example of an "If/then" scenario is: If I don't receive support from my close family, then I will seek guidance from a mentor or counselor.

5. Focus on the Action You Are Taking, Rather Than the Outcome

Pay attention to each task or decision you make, instead of thinking about the effects of the task or decision. Thinking about the effects can be a distraction from taking action, and in some cases it can discourage you from moving ahead with your plans. If you are intentional about what you desire and how you will go about achieving it, then the outcome will take care of itself. It is the process of self-improvement, not the product, which brings about the greatest amount of satisfaction.

Practicing Kaizen for Continual

Growth

Kaizen is a Japanese word that means continuous and incremental improvement. Similar to the 1% rule, practicing Kaizen is about taking small and intentional steps to achieve long-term growth. The concept originated at the end of the second World War when an American fellow named Edwards Deming went to Japan to help the Japanese redevelop their manufacturing industry. Since Deming was instrumental in improving the processes in the US manufacturing industry during the second World War, the Japanese had faith that he could bring new ideas to their manufacturing industry too.

Deming told the Japanese factory workers that to produce quality products, they needed to ask themselves a simple question: What small step can I take to improve the product or process? The workers applied Deming's advice and even turned it into a philosophy, which they named Kaizen. Since that time Japan has developed, evolved, implemented and utilized Kaizen as a driver for success in business throughout the country, truly making the concept her own. By practicing the philosophy of Kaizen, Japan was able to revitalize their manufacturing industry and become one of the leading manufacturers of the 20th century.

Kaizen is made up of two words. "Kai", meaning something that is good or valuable (this is also the root of the word "gai" in Ikigai), and "Zen", meaning change. Therefore, Kaizen means positive change. The philosophy of Kaizen has gained popularity in business and it often describes the process of eliminating waste and increasing efficiency. Kaizen can also be applied to personal development, and in this context, it refers to the continuous improvement you make in your life. Below are three strategies to help you practice Kaizen in your everyday life:

1. Ask Yourself Simple Questions to Arrive at Simple Answers

Instead of assuming that you know how to approach a certain task, ask yourself simple questions to gain understanding of the significance of what you are doing and the best approach in doing it. For example, you could ask yourself:

- Why is this task necessary? What is the purpose?

- What are the likely obstacles I may encounter?

- How will I sustain my motivation?

- What resources do I need to carry out the task?

- What are the risks of success?

- Where can I learn more about how to execute the task well?

2. Create a Simple Process

Knowing what you need to do is one thing, implementing the changes on a consistent basis is another. To make new habits and routines stick, you will need to create a process that you can follow each day or whenever you perform certain tasks. Creating a process will help you repeat certain tasks or behaviors in a consistent manner, on a regular basis. Ultimately, this will make it easier for your brain to learn the new tasks or behaviors so that they become permanent features of your lifestyle.

3. Visualize Positive Outcomes

It's your responsibility to keep yourself motivated as you make small improvements in your lifestyle. One way to keep yourself motivated is to regularly practice visualizing positive outcomes. Visualization is a powerful mental technique that helps you influence how you perceive things in your world. By feeding your mind specific ideals, images, and aspirations, you train yourself to think optimistically about your life and have confidence in your ability to achieve your goals. As a result, visualization can help you take on more risks, embrace change, and set high standards for your life.

Chapter Takeaways

- Resilience is the ability to survive under any circumstance. Since you were not born being resilient, you need to cultivate resilience over time by opening yourself to challenges, seeking support, and setting meaningful goals.

- Your brain is wired to remember what you write down. Thus, you can increase your chances of achieving your goals when you have them written down.

- Companies create mission statements to chart their path and help them track their progress. You can create a personal mission statement to outline what it is you hope to achieve and the value you intend to add in your life or the lives of others.

- Taking action requires you to figure out if you are doing the right thing. The right thing is always determined by action that leads you toward your goals. Remember that what you consider to be the right thing may not be the right thing for someone else.

- When seeking sustained improvements to your life, focus on making small positive changes that help you live and feel better.

Chapter 7:

Ikigai for Better Relationships

To be fully seen by somebody, then, and be loved anyhow - this is a human offering that can border on miraculous.

— Elizabeth Gilbert

What does it mean to truly be seen by someone?

In this chapter you will learn:

- The key ingredients that help to build purposeful relationships.

- Strategies for finding the kind of people who can accept you for who you are.

- Tips for communicating your needs with others.

Finding Purpose in Relationships

Relationships can add an incredible amount of value to your life. You might be an independent person capable of responding to your own needs, but there are still certain needs that you cannot fulfill on your own. For example, the need for belonging is something you can't fulfill by yourself—you need to be a part of a group, family, or team to feel a sense of belonging. It is so easy to get caught up in investing in your personal development that you forget to make investments into your relationships. But the truth is how others make you feel can influence how you feel about yourself.

Self-development could be seen as an isolated, lonely

process. However, Ikigai has a lot to do with the relationships in our lives. For a career-oriented person, their Ikigai might be networking with successful professionals and for a family-oriented person, their Ikigai might be spending quality time with loved ones. Therefore, the ability to cultivate healthy relationships can add to your overall sense of satisfaction within your life. When you feel as though you belong to a group of people, you will achieve psychological safety. Psychological safety is achieved when you are able to be open and vulnerable in front of others. Sharing your thoughts and emotions isn't threatening because you feel accepted by those you are communicating and connecting with.

Having psychological safety can improve your resilience during tough times. Instead of bottling up how you are feeling or trying to overcome challenges alone, you can turn to a community or network of people who can offer you emotional support, sound advice, practical skills or knowledge, and financial resources. In other words, even though you live an autonomous life, you never feel like you are walking your journey alone.

Many people neglect checking to see whether they have common interests or values with others before establishing relationships. The consequence is that these kinds of relationships aren't sustainable in the long-term. To build a purposeful relationship with someone, both you and the other person must be joined together by mutual or complementary interests, goals, skill sets and values. This does not necessarily mean you need to have the same interests, goals, skill sets and values, but they do need to be aligned. The more aligned and less in conflict they are, the more potential for the relationship to flourish. Without this alignment, neither you or the other person will be able find the relationship meaningful. With so many challenges and potential crises that arise to test the strength of relationships, those not built on mutual interests or values are likely to get swept away by the wind. This is because hard times are more likely to tear you and the other person apart than bring you closer together. Therefore, the glue in all your relationships should be your aligned interests and values.

In Chapter 3 we looked at the three drivers of Ikigai: passion, capacity and community. Just as you have worked to identify our own Ikigai, a similar method can be applied to finding your shared Ikigai with another person. Consider your relationship with another person or group of people and answer the following questions on passion, capacity and community.

Passion

- What are our shared interests?

- Do our passions align?

- Are we similarly passionate about things that compliment each other?

- Do our interests conflict?

- Do we have interest or passion toward each other?

- What interests do we have that differ?

Capacity

- What skills and talents are necessary for this relationship?

- What skills and talents does the other person possess?

- Are we similarly skilled?

- Do our skills and talents compliment each other?

- What is the potential for improvement in capacity?

Community

- Do you engage in similar social activities and communication styles?

- What do you think is the potential for the relationship?

- What do they think is the potential for the relationship?

- What value can you bring to each other?

- What are the potential barriers to connecting on a meaningful level?

- How do you network or community build?

Now assess and ground your answers. Identify similar and complementary aspects. Identify the potential obstacles, risks and areas of nonalignment. Grade their severity. Consider the adjustments that can be incorporated to mitigate points of nonalignment. Look at your own Ikigai. How does it align with theirs? How does it align with the above?

How to Find "Your People" and Build Your Tribe

When we feel accepted by those closest to us, it can

inspire us to fall deeply in love with ourselves and feel an immense amount of gratitude for those who allow us to be ourselves. People are often afraid of standing out, expressing how they feel, or thinking differently from others. Individuality can be replaced with blind collectivism, where the ideals of the group subvert those of the individual. However, it is important to keep in mind that living your own personal Ikigai does not need to be (and should not be) a solitary pursuit done in isolation.

Finding those who share your values while also encouraging freedom of expression and accepting you as you wish to be is an essential component to your success. These people will make up your tribe. A tribe can be a group or community of people with support and care for each other. They are joined together by common goals, interests, and values, and help each other through difficult times. There's an African proverb that says, "A family is like a forest, when you are outside it is dense, when you are inside you see that each tree has its place (Liles, 2021)." Inside your tribe, your thoughts, emotions, and lifestyle choices are accepted—and even celebrated—because you are treated like an individual who has value to offer the rest of the tribe.

Your tribe members celebrate your success and

encourage you to chase after your dreams because the happier and healthier you are, the more value you can add to the tribe. In other words, when you win, the rest of the tribe wins too. Sharing this kind of mindset removes the tendency to compete or make comparisons with others because each individual is seen to have a special place in the tribe. Considering how rare these kinds of bonds are between people, it is difficult to build a tribe. However, by staying true to yourself and living your life according to your own ideals, you can attract people who have similar views, values, and interests. Here are some tips on how to build your tribe:

1. **Create a list of qualities you look for in friendships (or professional relationships).** To find "your people" you need to know what kind of qualities they possess. Think about non-negotiable character traits, interests, or values you would like your tribe members to have. Be as specific as possible with your non-negotiables so that you attract the kind of people that meet your standard.

2. **Decide on what goals or activities bring you together.** There must be a certain goal or activity that causes you to meet up and spend time together. If you are creating a tribe with

your workmates then your goal could be career advancement or learning a new skill. If your tribe consists of a group of friends then your shared activity could be playing sports on weekends or doing family-focused activities together (if all of you are married or have children).

3. **Learn to trust your gut instinct about people.** It is possible to share similar interests and goals with someone but still feel uncomfortable around them. Your gut instinct will let you know who the right people are for you, and the kinds of people to avoid. The next time you meet a person, notice how you feel around them. Do you feel free to be yourself or are you guarded? Can you speak openly or do you feel like you are being judged?

4. **Look for your 1/3.** According to Andy Paige, a stylist on the network TLC, only 1/3 of people you come in contact with will love you for who you are, 1/3 may dislike you for no apparent reason, and another 1/3 will be indifferent about you. Don't be discouraged when you come across the 2/3 of people who won't accept you no matter how much you try to convince them. Focus your attention on the

1/3 that are your fierce supporters.

5. **Create meaningful rituals that keep you together.** Rituals are activities you perform in the same way repeatedly. Creating rituals with your tribe members can help you bond over activities, ensure that you spend enough time together, and keep the loyalty and affection between you. Rituals can be as simple as weekly meetings, sharing meals, going on holiday, or studying together.

How to Ask for What You Need in Relationships

As a human being you have needs. This doesn't automatically make you "needy." Neediness isn't the same as having and expressing your needs. A needy person relies on others to feel secure and safe. In other words, they refuse to stand on their own two feet and make decisions concerning their own life. This is different from a person who is capable of standing on their own two feet but seeks assistance from others.

The benefit of having a support system is that you have a few people you can seek whenever you need help. In exchange, they are able to come to you whenever they are in trouble or need assistance with something. Being confident in approaching your close friends and family for assistance isn't easy due to the stigma around asking for help. However, no human being can survive on their own, therefore at some point or another you will need to ask for assistance from others.

One of the things that can make asking for what you need tough is not being aware of what it is you need. You may not be able to express your need or be clear on what exactly you need help with. For example, if you are going through an emotionally difficult time, it may be hard for you to imagine how others might help you. You might be confused whether you need encouragement or just someone who can listen to you. It takes a great deal of self-awareness to be able to identify your lack and articulate how others might be able to help you overcome your challenge. Thus, it's better to first wrap your mind around your experience, understand the impact it has on you, and then finally look for ways others can help you cope.

Going through the process of developing and living your Ikigai simplifies the above. You've already put in the work to figure out what it is you want and need. You have developed a stronger sense of awareness. By working on your Ikigai you have the tools in hand. Now it's just a matter of expressing them clearly to get what you need from others.

One other factor that may make it hard to ask for what you need is the possibility of being rejected. It can be embarrassing to ask for something and be met with a no. Again, here we need to run a quick risk-analysis. Consider, what's worse: Asking for what you need and hearing a no or not seeking any assistance at all? Similar to failure, rejection is what you make it out to be. If you perceive rejection as a direct attack on who you are, then being rejected will hurt. However, if you choose to see rejection as redirection, then hearing no will simply mean you need to ask someone else. There are many reasons why people aren't able to assist us in times of need. Most of these reasons don't even have to do with us. Therefore, by making rejection less about you, it can feel less overwhelming.

Since relationships can influence your Ikigai, and vise-versa, it is important to learn to voice your needs so you get the most value out of every relationship. Without communicating your needs, your partner, friend, or colleague won't know how to help you or how to make the relationship meaningful for you. It can be easy to pass off your needs as being trivial, but this isn't true. When your needs go unmet you can eventually feel resentful or taken for granted by others. Therefore, for the health and harmony of your relationships, it's worth communicating what you need.

So how can you learn to be better at asking for what you need? Here are five steps that you can follow:

1. Decide That You Deserve Your Needs to Be Met

Sometimes, what makes it challenging to ask for help is the belief that we are not worthy of it. However, if you are in healthy relationships, chances are that others will be more than happy to assist you. Learn to make positive assumptions about receiving the help you need. Tell yourself that there is bound to be at least one person who can meet your needs.

2. Accept That Asking for Help Is a Risk

When you ask for help, you can hear one of two answers: no or yes. People are entitled to say no to your request when they are not able or willing to meet your needs (the same applies when you aren't able to help another person). Ideally, you will want to hear yes all of the time, but that won't always be the case. Approach people with the understanding that they have the opportunity to choose to help you or not.

3. Be Specific About What You Need

It is difficult to receive help when you can't articulate

what you need. Moreover, clarifying what your needs are can help you approach the right people for help. Take some time to think about your problem and decide on what you aren't able to resolve on your own. Approach people knowing the role you would like them to play in resolving the matter.

4. Consider the Right People to Ask

Since asking for what you need makes you vulnerable and can leave you feeling exposed, it's important to consider the right people to ask for help. Bear in mind that you may need to consult a few people before you find someone who can help you. Consider whether you need expert advice or encouragement from someone you know personally. You can also consider the best people to ask for certain resources. For instance, some people may be able to help you financially while others are better off giving you their time.

5. Generously Offer Help to Others

What keeps healthy relationships going is reciprocity. Each person takes a turn in being the receiver and the giver. In times when you don't need help from others, focus on being the giver and generously offering your support. This will make it easier for others to jump at the opportunity of helping you when you are in need. Remember that there are more valuable things to offer people than money. Perhaps the most valuable thing you can give to someone is your time. Block out time in your calendar to spend with those close to you or those with whom you would like to be closer. This will show them how much you appreciate your relationship with them. When you can't offer your time, consider offering your appreciation instead. Saying phrases like, "Thank you," "I appreciate you," and "I am here if you need me," can go a long way into making others feel connected.

Chapter Takeaways

- You can find purpose in your relationships when you share mutual interests and values with others.

- It can take time and patience to find people who accept you for who you are and can support you on your journey. Nonetheless, by being yourself you can attract like-minded people who won't make you feel judged for being yourself.

- Asking for what you need in relationships does not need to come across as being needy. Neediness is the dependency on others, which is different from communicating how others might support you.

- Hearing no is tough, but changing how you perceive rejection can make asking for help feel less intimidating. Start to see rejection as redirection, not an attack on who you are as a person.

Conclusion

You cannot swim for new horizons until you have courage to lose sight of the shore.

— William Faulkner

It has become more important now than ever to examine who you are. Each day, you are bombarded with images, ideas, and beliefs that seek to control the narrative of your life. You are told by friends, family, the media, organizations, and interest groups what to think, how to feel, and the kinds of goals to achieve.

But in reality, there is no one who can understand you better than you understand yourself.

You can be the expert when it comes to sensing what you need at any given time. You know what you like and dislike by simply listening to yourself and noticing how you react to certain things. Therefore, when it comes to discovering your purpose, there is no better person to consult than YOU.

Although Ikigai is a traditional Japanese philosophy, it has been adopted by many different cultures across the world, and used for career advancement, achieving good health, and personal development. While there are many different interpretations of the meaning of Ikigai, perhaps the best way to describe it is the "reason and purpose in life."

What is your reason and purpose in life? Were you able to find it while reading this book? Or maybe you still have a long way to go before you can confidently say you have discovered it. Finding your Ikigai is a life-long journey that has many twists and turns. Furthermore, at each stage of your life, what you consider Ikigai can be different. In other words, your Ikigai isn't a single thing that you live by for the rest of your life. Instead, it is a theme that continues to evolve from one life stage to another, with the more life experience and growth you acquire.

The intention of this book was to introduce you to the concept of Ikigai and show you the various ways you can apply it to your life. The hope was that through reading each chapter, you would realize that Ikigai is more than materialistic gain or achieving certain goals. Certainly, achieving goals is part of Ikigai but you can still find purpose in simply being yourself. It is enough of an achievement to discover yourself and live the rest of your life expressing who you are. Knowing who you are is the ultimate success in life.

Throughout the book, the word "purpose" was mentioned a lot. This is because "purpose" is the closest Western translation of Ikigai. But remember that how you define purpose is subjective and doesn't need to look or feel like what you see in your environment. Your purpose doesn't need to make you money, although it can. The core criteria is that it is something that resonates with your heart and helps you feel grateful for being alive.

As a reminder, if you haven't yet received your FREE copy of the Practical Ikigai Discovery Journal, I highly recommend it. It is a fantastic companion to this this book and a helpful tool for your journey.

You can purchase a paperback copy on Amazon here:

https://mybook.to/ikigaijournal

Or to get instant access to the free digital copy just go to:

hellomulberryavenue.com/ikigaidiscovery

Inside the book you will find:

- Writing prompts to explore your IKIGAI

- The core concepts described in this book

- Activities to help you better understand and drive yourself

References

Ashman, J. (2020, April 20). *Japan's "Kodawari" and my next job.* LinkedIn. https://www.linkedin.com/pulse/japans-kodawari-my-next-job-jim-ashman

Ask Any Difference. (n.d.). *Difference between talent and skill (with table).* Ask Any Difference. https://askanydifference.com/difference-between-talent-and-skill/

Balslov, L. (2020, May 27). *What is Kodawari?* Exploring Kodawari. https://exploringkodawari.blog/what-is-kodawari/

Barry, A. (2020, February 14). *Ikigai and the importance of being curious.* Curious Lion. https://curiouslionlearning.com/ikigai-and-the-importance-of-being-curious/

Begin, B. (2018, June 18). *Achieve your goals faster with the 1% rule.* The Fearless Man. https://www.thefearlessman.com/achieve-your-goals-faster-with-the-1-rule/

Berardi, F. B. (n.d.). *Franco Bifo Berardi quotes.* Good Reads. https://www.goodreads.com/author/show/4449492.Franco_Bifo_Berardi

Beuttner, D. (2010, October 19). *The blue zones: Lessons for living longer from the people who've lived the longest.* Amazon. https://www.amazon.com/Blue-Zones-Lessons-Living-Longest/dp/1426207557

Brooke. (2018, October 30). *"Kaizen" = The key to self-improvement.* The Health Investment. https://thehealthinvestment.com/kaizen-self-improvement/

Brown, H. J. (n.d.). *H. Jackson Brown Jr. quotes.* Good Reads. https://www.goodreads.com/author/show/33394.H_Jackson_Brown_Jr_

Camacho-Ruiz, J. (2017, September 19). *How to increase your value to others.* JJR Marketing. https://jjrmarketing.com/how-to-increase-your-value-to-others/

Castrillon, C. (2020, March 8). *5 Steps to turn passion into profit.* Forbes. https://www.forbes.com/sites/carolinecastrillon/2020/03/08/5-steps-to-turn-passion-into-profit/?sh=1b448b12700b

Chernoff, M. (2010, August 16). *How to build your tribe – finding "your people."* Marc and Angel Hack Life. https://www.marcandangel.com/2010/08/16/how-to-build-your-tribe-finding-your-people/

Das, S. (2021, August 5). *The Japanese philosophy of "Kodawari" - Great minds think alike.* Linkedin. https://www.linkedin.com/pulse/japanese-philosophy-kodawari-great-minds-think-alike-swarup-das

Davis, T. (n.d.). *Taking action: 8 Key steps for acting on your dreams.* The Berkeley Well-Being Institute. https://www.berkeleywellbeing.com/taking-action.html

Dayman, L. (2020, January 15). *Ikigai: The Japanese concept of finding purpose in life.* Savvy Tokyo. https://savvytokyo.com/ikigai-japanese-concept-finding-purpose-life/

Economy, P. (2018, February 28). *This is the way you need to write down your goals for faster success.* Inc; Inc. https://www.inc.com/peter-economy/this-is-way-you-need-to-write-down-your-goals-for-faster-success.html

Esfahani, E. (2017, January 11). *The secret to a meaningful life is meaningful relationships.* The Gottman Institute. https://www.gottman.com/blog/secret-meaningful-life-meaningful-relationships/

Fauziah. (2017, May 22). *7 Simple ways to apply Kaizen for personal growth.* Indoindians. https://www.indoindians.com/7-simple-ways-to-apply-kaizen-for-personal-growth/

Forsey, C. (2021, January 25). *Here's how to write an impressive personal mission statement [examples and template].* Hubspot. https://blog.hubspot.com/marketing/personal-mission-statement

Frankl, V. E. (n.d.). *A quote by Viktor E. Frankl.* Good Reads. https://www.goodreads.com/quotes/8144491-between-stimulus-and-response-there-is-a-space-in-that

Gaines, J. (2020, November 17). *The philosophy of Ikigai: 3 Examples about finding purpose.* Positive Psychology. https://positivepsychology.com/ikigai/

Gilbert, E. (n.d.). *Elizabeth Gilbert quote.* Good Reads. https://www.goodreads.com/author/show/11679.Elizabeth_Gilbert

Gilmore, H. (2021, January 7). *Life crafting: Creating a plan to live your best life.* ABA Parent Training. https://www.abaparenttraining.com/home/2021/1/7/life-crafting-creating-a-plan-to-live-your-best-life

Greene, B. (2019, August 7). *The psychology of writing down goals.* New Tech Seattle. https://www.newtechnorthwest.com/the-psychology-of-writing-down-goals/

Hendriksen, E. (2019). *5 Ways to overcome your fear of failure.* Psychology Today.

https://www.psychologytoday.com/us/blog/how-be-yourself/201910/5-ways-overcome-your-fear-failure

Herrera, T. (2021, February 6). Remember: What you do is not who you are. *The New York Times.* https://www.nytimes.com/2021/02/06/style/work-life-balance-tips-pandemic.html

Howard, L. (2017, May 22). *How to feel more comfortable asking for what you need in a relationship.* Bustle. https://www.bustle.com/p/how-to-feel-more-comfortable-asking-for-what-you-need-in-a-relationship-59044

Huebner, T. (n.d.). *Knowing yourself is the beginning of wisdom.* Emyth. https://www.emyth.com/inside/knowing-yourself-is-the-beginning-of-wisdom#:~:text=Aristotle%20said%20%E2%80%9Cknowing%20yourself%20is

Ikigai Consultancy. (2019, April 25). *Finding Ikigai.* Medium. https://medium.com/@ikigai.consultancy/finding-ikigai-c1fc4c70f58f

Ikigai Living. (2019, August 1). *What is the kanji for ikigai?* Ikigai Living. https://ikigai-living.com/what-is-the-kanji-for-ikigai/

Ikigai Tribe. (2019, July 23). *Ikigai misunderstood and the origin of the Ikigai venn diagram.* Ikigai Tribe. https://ikigaitribe.com/ikigai/ikigai-misunderstood/

Ikigai Tribe. (2020, January 19). *Interview with Ken Mogi on the 5 pillars of Ikigai.* Ikigai Tribe. https://ikigaitribe.com/podcasts/podcast06/

Illing, S. (2019, March 16). *Why are millennials burned out? Capitalism.* Vox. https://www.vox.com/2019/2/4/18185383/millennials-capitalism-burned-out-malcolm-harris

Kerpen, D. (2014, March 27). *15 Inspiring quotes on passion (get back to what you love).* Inc; Inc. https://www.inc.com/dave-kerpen/15-quotes-on-passion-to-inspire-a-better-life.html

Kowalski, K. (2019, May 22). *The truth about Ikigai: Definitions, diagrams and myths.* Sloww. https://www.sloww.co/ikigai/

Krull, E. (2021, July 26). *How to politely ask for help when you really need it: 7 Steps.* Join Cake. https://www.joincake.com/blog/ask-for-help/

Kyte, J. (2014, November 3). *The 1 percent principle: The foolproof way to reach your goals.* Woman and Home Magazine. https://www.womanandhome.com/health-and-wellbeing/the-1-percent-principle-the-foolproof-way-to-reach-your-goals-103554/

Lee, M.-A., & Kawachi, I. (2019). The keys to happiness: Associations between personal values regarding core life domains and happiness in South Korea. *PLOS ONE*, *14*(1), e0209821. https://doi.org/10.1371/journal.pone.0209821

Liles, M. (2021, May 4). *150 of the Best African Proverbs About Life, Love and Family That Are Full of Poetic Wisdom*. Parade: Entertainment, Recipes, Health, Life, Holidays. https://parade.com/1100530/marynliles/african-proverbs/

M, J. (2021, November 6). *Small steps, big results: How the 1% rule will change your life. The Qosh*. The Qosh. https://www.theqosh.com/finance-career/the-one-percent-rule-small-steps-big-results/

Marx, O. (2017, April 20). *Why you should practice the art of life crafting*. Medium. https://medium.com/@orianmarx/why-you-should-practice-the-art-of-life-crafting-9de4d8aa2b43

Mind Tools Content Team. (2009). Overcoming fear of failure: *Facing your fear of moving forward*. Mind Tools. https://www.mindtools.com/pages/article/fear-of-failure.htm

Mitsuhashi, Y. (2017, August 7). *Ikigai: A Japanese*

concept to improve work and life. BBC. https://www.bbc.com/worklife/article/20170807-ikigai-a-japanese-concept-to-improve-work-and-life

Nagda, H. (n.d.). *Do what you love quotes (81 quotes).* Good Reads. https://www.goodreads.com/quotes/tag/do-what-you-love

Nguyen, A. (2018, July 3). *Council post: Three practical steps to truly uncover your natural talents.* Forbes. https://www.forbes.com/sites/forbescoachescouncil/2019/07/03/three-practical-steps-to-truly-uncover-your-natural-talents/?sh=7261b7d41082

O'neil, T. (2013). *The 1% principle.* HarperCollins Publishers.

Pietrangelo, A. (2020, September 30). *What is a fear of success?* Healthline. https://www.healthline.com/health/anxiety/fear-of-success#definition

PsychAlive. (2015, August 28). *Finding yourself: A guide to finding your true self.* PsychAlive. https://www.psychalive.org/finding-yourself/

Puigcerver, H. G. (n.d.). *Ikigai quotes by Hector Garcia Puigcerver.* Good Reads. https://www.goodreads.com/work/quotes/48995874-

ikigai-los-secretos-de-jap-n-para-una-vida-larga-y-feliz

Rampton, J. (2018, November 16). *The 5 things in life that are more valuable than money*. John Rampton. https://www.johnrampton.com/the-5-things-in-life-that-are-more-valuable-than-money/

Ribeiro, M. (2019, July 4). *How to become mentally strong: 14 Strategies for building resilience*. Positive Psychology. https://positivepsychology.com/mentally-strong/

Romer, C. (2021, February 8). *The importance of community*. Vail Valley Partnership. https://www.vailvalleypartnership.com/2021/02/the-importance-of-community/

Sarokin, D. (2020, October 9). *How to define your passion in life*. Chron. https://work.chron.com/define-passion-life-10132.html

Seetubtim, M. (2017, February 6). *How to turn your passion into your life's work*. The Happiness Planner®. https://thehappinessplanner.com/blogs/wisdom/how-to-turn-your-passion-into-your-life-s-work

Selig, M. (2016, March 9). *Know yourself? 6 Specific ways to know who you are*. Psychology Today. https://www.psychologytoday.com/us/blog/changepower/201603/know-yourself-6-specific-ways-know-who-you-are

Shinkai, J. (2020, July 7). *Ikigai myth busting.* Jennifer Shinkai. https://jennifershinkai.com/2020/07/07/ikigai-myth-busting/

Sil, A. (2016, June 21). *Human abilities: Meaning and nature.* Psychology Discussion. https://www.psychologydiscussion.net/educational-psychology/human-abilities/human-abilities-meaning-and-nature-educational-psychology/1914

Spacey, J. (2018, November 11). *35 Examples of ability.* Simplicable. https://simplicable.com/new/ability

Spoto, J. (2021, October 20). Does more money make us happier? *The Lowell Sun.* https://www.lowellsun.com/2021/10/20/does-more-money-make-us-happier/

The Economic Times. (2015, July 13). *Steve Jobs' 14 most inspiring quotes.* The Economic Times. https://economictimes.indiatimes.com/people/steve-jobs-14-most-inspiring-quotes/be-a-yardstick-of-quality/slideshow/48051258.cms

The Growth Reactor. (2021, May 1). *80 Best fire quotes to light your inner flame.* The Growth Reactor. https://www.thegrowthreactor.com/fire-quotes/

The Week Staff. (2015, January 12). *7 Ways to quickly*

become a master at anything. The Week. https://theweek.com/articles/448231/7-ways-quickly-become-master-anything

Thompson, B. (2021, July 21). *What is passion and what it means to have passion.* Lifehack. https://www.lifehack.org/articles/lifestyle/what-means-have-passion.html

Tilly, M. (2017, December 7). *What Ikigai means and how to find yours.* The Institute of You. https://instituteofyou.org/what-ikigai-means-and-how-to-find-yours/

Turner, I. (2017, October 14). *Mental toughness - The "grit" behind the 4Cs.* Linkedin. https://www.linkedin.com/pulse/mental-toughness-grit-behind-4cs-ian-turner

Valentine, M. (2014, November 17). *6 Awesome Zen stories that will teach you important life lessons.* Buddhaimonia. https://buddhaimonia.com/blog/zen-stories-important-life-lessons

Made in United States
Orlando, FL
09 May 2023

32928630R10114